W9-BLS-334

# A Joyful Mother of Children

# A Joyful Mother of Children

Help Despite the Hassles for Mothers of Young Children

Linda J. Eyre

Bookcraft · Salt Lake City, Utah

Copyright © 1983 by Linda J. Eyre

All rights reserved. This book or any part thereof may not be reproduced in any form whatsoever, whether by graphic, visual, electronic, filming, microfilming, tape recording, or any other means, without the prior written permission of Bookcraft, Inc., except in the case of brief passages embodied in critical reviews and articles.

Library of Congress Catalog Card Number: 83-70692
ISBN O-88494-482-4

**4th Printing, 1987**

Lithographed in the United States of America
PUBLISHERS PRESS
Salt Lake City, Utah

To my Heavenly Father, who taught me to
learn by experience

To Mr. Munk, who taught me to
write by experience

And to my parents, husband, and children,
who gave me experience

# Contents

# Preface

*F*or my birthday last year my husband gave me Wednesday. By that I mean that on the Wednesdays when he's in town, he comes home by midmorning and I go to the office or the woods or a park—to write. Because of this greatest of all gifts, time, I have been able to finish this project, which I many times thought would be impossible because there simply was no time. Through it all my loyal husband, Richard, has been my prodder, my baby sitter, my encourager, my advisor, and my best friend.

I have been formulating the ideas in this book for many years. What started out to be a record for my own use, and to give our daughters a sense of the monumental task and importance of mothering, has found its way to a publisher.

Much love and appreciation go to a caring, encouraging husband and to all the Eyre children—so far: Saren, twelve; Shawni, eleven; Joshua, nine; Saydi, seven; Jonah, five; Talmadge, three; Noah, two; and "?," who will join us a month or two after this book is published. Thanks also go to my typist and friend, Corry DeMille, and to many other friends who have inspired me to be better through the exchange of ideas and by their own shining examples.

Most of us have had absolutely no formal training as mothers, other than what we got from baby sitting or helping with younger children in the family. (My youngest and only sister, Lenna, is thirteen months younger than I and didn't care much for my "baby sitting" ability.) Often the most help we can get from anywhere is a sympathetic (or pathetic) look on the face of the lady in the grocery store who sees a baby in an infant seat and two other little ones crawling in and out of the moving basket and says, "My, don't you have your hands full!"

Although there are specific things that we can do to be better mothers, I am not attempting to say that we can all become "super moms," or that we should try to be better mothers than our friends or neighbors. My hope is that the ideas herein may create in each reader a desire to be her *own* best. Because of varying talents and gifts and children, each person's best will be unique.

With all the distractions of our fast-moving era, with its beckoning to love the things of the world, with the unrelenting demands of a house that needs constant scrubbing and scraping, with car-pools that need "running" and Church responsibilities that beg attention, with, in some cases, the demands of a part- or full-time job—may we remember the story of Martha and Mary. (Luke 10:38-41.) We need to take time to quit fussing over the comparatively unimportant details of life and choose "that good part"—our children.

I am sorry to inform you that although most people who write books consider themselves experts on their subjects, my case is quite the opposite. I am still struggling like everyone else. Our children still have arguments, and I still lose my temper, despite the joy we feel as a family.

The writing of this book, however, has helped me to be a better mother, for which I am grateful. It is my fondest wish that it may spark ideas in the minds of other mothers, and that we might all realize more fully not only the divinity and responsibility of being mothers, but also the true joy—that we might each become "a joyful mother of children" (Psalm 113:9).

# Chapter One

# The Greatest Career

Normally the last thing I would consider doing during a play in New York City would be to boo or hiss because I disagreed with what was being said—but it was all I could do to keep my mouth shut in this case.

The star of the show was playing an aspiring songwriter who was having a great deal of trouble feeling confident about her lyrics for a new song. Finally, in exasperation, she exclaimed (in essence), "I just can't make this come out right! It's absolutely no good! I can't do anything! I might just as well quit and go to work in some day-care center!" The insinuation was that the people with the least talent, skill, and imagination should be put to work teaching the preschoolers.

One of the saddest mistakes of our time is the misunderstanding of motherhood. For years, in this age of equal rights and liberation, the press and media have tried to convince us that the most demeaning job that can be found anywhere belongs to the young woman who is "doomed" to stay home and tend young children—that the place we used to think of as a refuge has become a prison!

Often, even when it is not financially compulsory, the young mother is wooed by the excitement of a job outside the home, complete with an orderly office, meaningful adult relationships, and tangible monetary rewards. She diligently finds an acceptable day-care center or suitable baby sitter and can hardly wait to get out into the working world so that she can afford a few more of life's luxuries and not have to rely on her husband totally for support. Somehow money and freedom from the cares of home become the goal. (Please understand that I am not referring to cases of absolute need—such as single mothers or families with situations of financial crisis.)

At a meeting of the National Council of Women, probably the oldest and most recognized women's organization in America, I heard a young woman, Elizabeth Nichols, author of *The Coming Matriarchy*, speak to a large group of prestigious women. She suggested that the future family will be "rotational," meaning that not only mothers and fathers but also children will rotate from unit to unit until they find satisfactory settings for particular times in their lives. Food preparation was referred to as almost a thing of the past because of all the modern computerized conveniences, thus, the woman could spend much more time outside the home. "When the woman is granted equal financial rewards for her work," she said, "then she will have her own financial base and at last she will be able to marry for love instead of money."

I stirred uneasily in my seat and looked around to see if I could read the faces in the room. *Do they really believe that?* I thought as I saw a few nods, a few raised eyebrows, but mostly inscrutable stares.

Growing more and more apprehensive as the time went on, I heard other speakers say such things as, "The greatest need in America today is for quality, twenty-four-hour-a-day child-care centers so that mothers can be free to work day or night." I began to wonder if our society is working to live or living to work.

The theme of the conference was "Women and Work: Families and the Future." But so much was being said about women and work, and so little about real families. I was anxious partly because that very afternoon, in front of this same noble body of women, I was to give a two-minute response to a special citation I had been selected to receive. I was one of six women under the age of thirty-five who were being cited for outstanding achievement in their careers. The careers of the other five recipients spanned from treasurer of the United States to publisher of *Harper's Magazine*. My award, as nearly as I could tell, was being given for my bearing and teaching children.

The statement I was going to make, which my husband and I had carefully worked out just a few hours before, was the exact opposite of what had been said up to that point.

That afternoon, at the moment my name was called, I don't mind saying that I was scared. I believed what I had to say, however, and say it I would. As I stood listening to the person reading my citation, I took heart a bit when she came to the part that said, "She is the mother of seven children." An audible gasp and a buzz that went through the audience prevented the reader momentarily from continuing. I saw many smiles and several looks that seemed to say, "You must be from Mars." Still, I could not tell if the smiles were of amusement or encouragement, and when the reader had finished and I had received the citation from Governor Cary of New York, I stepped to the podium and said the following:

"I feel today a little like a three-year-old boy that I observed on a busy London street a couple of years ago. His mother was reprimanding him, tugging him along by the arm, and the boy was crying and protesting. I quickened my pace and, as I got within earshot, I heard the boy say, 'I didn't did it, Mom. I didn't did it.' The mother reached full agitation, picked the boy up to eye level, and roared back at him: 'You didn't *do* it!' The little boy stopped crying, looked wide-eyed at his mother, and said, 'Then who did?'

"Today, in the presence of such outstanding women, I am saying to myself in the words of that little boy, *I didn't did it—didn't do anything worthy of such an honor.*

"I am, however, pleased to accept this citation in behalf of the many women who, as the program says, make contributions under relatively obscure conditions—particularly those women who make their main contribution as mothers, as cultivators of America's next generation.

"You know, all of us here, whether conscious of it or not, have multiple careers. We are all involved in more than one thing. In some careers the bottom line is profit. In others it is productivity. Those of us who write have a bottom line of publication, and in the arts we like to think we aim at perfection. In teaching, the bottom line is pupils and preparedness. But there is another career, and I think it is the most demanding and multifaceted career of all, in which the bottom line is people—little people: our children.

"We have embarked, my husband and I, over the last few years, on an effort to popularize parenting. Our work at the White House, our writing, and our national network of parents' groups have aimed at helping people realize that our most significant and serious problems, both personal and societal, have their roots in our homes, and that parenting, when it is pursued seriously and thoughtfully, is not only life's most important career, but its most joyful and fulfilling career. Thank you."

The response was overwhelming. The applause told me that the audience believed what I said, or at least wanted to believe it. Mothering is a career—the hardest and the best!

In a reception line afterward many clamored over our two oldest children, who were with us, and warmly and sincerely congratulated me. I felt that, through me, they were congratulating all of you: you dedicated mothers who have devoted your lives to a career at home rearing a family.

If we as mothers believe that our relationships with God and our families are our highest priority in life, if we regard our children as people that Heavenly Father entrusted to us to nurture and teach and prepare for their own parenting, then we must approach our position as being of the highest importance. It is an awesome responsibility. In these days when we hear so much of women's rights, it is time we turned our thoughts to women's responsibilities.

Of course, it is important for a wife to support her husband in his endeavors to earn a living and progress in his career. But if we look at the children and the relationship established in the home as having the highest priority, then it is really the husband who is supporting the wife. He is providing the means whereby the family can have what they need to grow and learn in a well-organized home amidst the woes of a complicated society. If the husband can provide the support system, then it is a great privilege for the wife to be able to stay home and create a plan to produce an atmosphere for learning and loving.

I love to think that C. S. Lewis agrees. He said: "Homemaking is surely in reality the most important work in the world. What do ships, railways, mine cars and government, etc., exist for except that people may be warmed and safe in their own home? . . . [The homemaker's] is the job for which all others exist." (As quoted in Tamara Allred, *From Deadlines to Diapers* [Provo, Utah: Liberty Press, 1982], inside front cover.)

In a CBS radio interview taped during National Family Week one November, the interviewer, who had heard me expound on the importance of viewing motherhood as the greatest of all careers, asked, "Do you mean to say that you'd rather be at home with your kids than to be the president of IBM?"

Although I'd never pondered that question, I felt sure of my unequivocal yes.

Managing a home and family is no less demanding or time consuming than running a large corporation or pursuing any other career. The most successful homes are run by mothers who take their careers as seriously as any top executive. However, instead of dealing with making a product profitable, we deal with making profit of human lives.

It is true that we acquire children in a different way than we would acquire a company. And we are amateurs at the business of parenthood. One morning we wake up with a pink, wrinkled little bundle beside the hospital bed and presto! we are parents.

However, the development of lovely, joyful, responsible children doesn't just happen accidentally, any more than a successful corporation just happens. A unified, organized, progressing family requires a unified, organized, progressive plan! Setting goals and producing a plan are just as essential to a mother and father as to a good company.

Just as it takes a goal and plan to become a good tennis player or pianist, and then time and dedication to the plan and hard, concentrated effort and practice, so it is with being a good and happy mother.

And just think of the rewards—and the results! As Winston Churchill said, "We shape our homes and then our homes shape us."

## More Challenging Than We Could Have Known

There was once a wise king who wanted his people to understand the essence of life. He called together all his wise men and charged them to go out into the world and bring together the things that would help his people most to understand life. This they did with fervor, as they loved their king and wanted very much to please him.

After some time, they came back with eight volumes of carefully thought-out material which they proudly presented to the king. "Oh, my, no," exclaimed the king when he saw the volumes. "This is much too complicated. My people will never take the time to read all this! Simplify this and bring it back as quickly as possible."

Once again the wise men strove to please their king, and within a month had condensed their work to one volume, which was proudly delivered. With regret the king again reported that the volume was much too long and must be condensed. "I only want the very essence," admonished the king as the dejected wise men again set out to accomplish their task.

After much struggle they returned to the king with a one-page document, which once again was rejected as still too complicated and diversified. "I need something that even the simplest souls can understand," the king reminded as they trudged off to give it one more try.

A week later they presented the king with a scroll that contained only one sentence, and were overjoyed to see the king's wide smile as he read the statement, looked up, and said, "This is it—the essence of life in common, everyday language!" Looking reverently at the paper, he read it to his subjects. It said, "There Ain't No Free Lunch!"

So also is the essence of motherhood: It's hard! In fact, it is harder than any of us could have guessed.

As I gazed into the eyes of our seventh child, only twenty-eight days old, I couldn't help but feel the same awe I had felt with the first and with every one in between. It was just at the point in time when the glaze was beginning to clear from his eyes and he had stopped seeing the angels and started seeing us.

Yes, I think *awesome* is the word to describe this fresh, new spirit, so sweet and clean despite the spewings out both ends of the awkward, cumbersome body. He is awesome also because of the things he represents. I knew then, however—with this seventh child much better than I had with the first—what to expect.

I have to smile when I look back on those rather naive times most of us have before we become mothers for the first time. Oh my, the daydreams I used to have!

*What fun it will be,* I thought, *to have someone call me Mommy, how exciting to sew dresses for my little girls and knickers for my little boys, and how terrific to have a real excuse to leave a boring church meeting. How wonderful to have the family playing musical instruments together, each on his own part!* My list of exciting things about having a family of my own went on. *Just think of the lovely furniture, the rooms neat and orderly, and the gourmet meals I will prepare,* I mused.

When that first sweet baby finally came, I suddenly realized some things I hadn't thought of before. She had to be fed every two or three hours. I worried constantly about whether or not she got enough to eat because she cried before *and* after I fed her. She certainly eliminated the time I could spend with my husband and friends, because I was up all night feeding and changing. I felt like a zombie in the morning—irritable and touchy.

The sacrifices changed, but they never ended as the child grew. As two more children joined the ranks, I realized that sewing little dresses was not exactly the bliss I'd envisioned. While I tried to sew, the baby screamed, the two-year-old dumped the pins on the floor every fifteen minutes, and the four-year-old cut up the pattern pieces I wasn't using.

Not only that, but as the children grew old enough to begin music training, those dreams of chamber music were clouded by the fact that the end result required endless hours of getting up early, of training the children to practice, and of developing patience and living with a battered ear. We went through years of screeching violins, and of big tears splashing on the piano keys because, to quote Shawni, "I don't get this!" or, to quote Saren, "Oh, Mom, why do I have to practice?"

After the first two months in the foyer at church and the next several years trying to keep the children reverent and quiet during church meetings I thought, *What a blessing it would be just to sit back and meditate and bask in the words of the speaker, any speaker. What a treat it would be to just sit and listen!*

The visions of a spotless house with the beds always made and the bathroom taps always polished melted into the realization that getting children to "think orderly" was one of the greatest challenges of my life. I found that it takes concentration and commitment to get things done in the morning.

As I struggled out the door to run an errand with three little ones stumbling all over each other, and noticed the mud, toothpaste, and play dough all over the bathroom taps, sink, and walls, I remember thinking, *Thank goodness for "selected neglect"!*

I found that the laundry never ends and the kitchen always needs to be cleared and cleaned, no matter how many times a day it is done.

I realized that the kids wouldn't eat the gourmet meals I fixed. The typical reaction to the slaved-over hollandaise sauce is, "What is this strange stuff?" Often, in exasperation, the next night I resort to fish sticks or hot dogs.

As the table gets more crowded with bodies, the visions of peaceful meals—beginning with a quiet devotional, followed by each person talking about his day or something interesting he found or saw—fade into the realities of an argument about who is sitting where, and the wailing of the three-year-old under the table because she doesn't *want* to eat her main course before she has her dessert. Somebody is always crying about an "accidental" elbow in the ribs or mourning over spilled milk.

The grand idea of every child being perfect as a result of great upbringing crumbles a bit when your six-year-old, with a fascination for scissors, shows up with six pairs he confiscated from the school supply. (He's already used them to cut little brother's hair.) Hope deteriorates further when the three-year-old takes his friend into his room to "play" and comes out half an hour later having methodically torn off the wallpaper in hundreds of pretty little pieces as far up as little hands can reach.

I also didn't realize that motherhood would include listening to the delighted squeals of an eighteen-month-old and a three-

year-old in the back of the station wagon, only to look into the rearview mirror and realize that their delight was from watching the newly purchased bushel of peaches bounce and spatter down the freeway as they popped them through the opening in the rear window one by one.

Nor did I realize how many times a day I would have to change a one-year-old who was doggedly determined to sit *in* the toilet to play—no matter what else was in there!

I would never have dreamed that some day I would be careless enough to leave the car running and dash into the grocery store to get some milk, only to look up and see the checkstand lady chasing my car across the parking lot with our three-year-old at the wheel and our delighted eight-month-old as passenger.

The Perils of Pauline could not compare to the exciting life of an everyday mother.

Just as I reach the breaking point, into my head will pop the scripture: "All these things shall give thee experience" (D&C 122:7), or the words of the king's wise men, "There ain't no free lunch!"

## And More Rewarding Than We Could Have Imagined

My mind flashed back to the wriggling baby in my arms. My back ached and my head pounded from a hard day of feeding, washing, and refereeing, but I realized as I looked into those eyes that even though mothering was different than I had envisioned, it was *better!*

I relaxed, settled back a little, closed my eyes, and remembered that life is not one exhilarating joy after another. But the occasional moments of real joy make us able to chalk up the rest to experience.

Who can explain the feeling of sheer joy that comes from watching a baby's first breath? Suddenly all the discomforts of nausea, the awkwardness of getting in and out of cars, and the inconvenience of not being able to tie your shoes or even see your feet, of having grown out of all your clothes and wondering if you'll ever look normal again, fade into the joy of having brought a new person into the world.

The satisfaction, much fuller than you could have known, comes when you see two little girls, obviously feeling beautiful, skipping off to their dance review in the costumes you've made (with their help).

What fun it is to see your two-year-old finally fold his arms and sit through the opening prayer almost to the end—quietly—and to watch your three-year-old actually try to draw his rendition of Jesus during church services and to know that, at least for a few minutes, his mind is in the right place!

How exciting it is to hear Daddy say to Saren one morning after her violin practicing: "My gosh, Saren, was that you? I thought the radio was on"; and to see the proud yet humble little smile as she realizes that he really means it..

The wonder and great feelings of satisfaction that come *because* of the struggle are beyond description. I am sometimes overwhelmed when I see children really ready for school, with teeth brushed, beds made, practicing done.

Then there is the occasional meal when everything goes right. After a meaningful family prayer, everyone explains his happy day, and no one cries over the spilled milk.

What satisfaction there is in seeing our six-year-old understand repentance a bit better as he takes the confiscated scissors back to his teacher and, after a full three minutes of silence, manages to say, "I'm sorry, will you forgive me?" How great it is to see the relief—and yes, even joy—in his face as he walks to his desk with a little smile, the weight of the world obviously lifted from his shoulders.

It seems that the blessings of motherhood never cease (I guess because the hard times never do either), and the joy is so much more than we could have expected.

The effect that our mothering has is also more long-term than most of us would imagine. I cite the example of one brave colonial woman: "One of the most remarkable examples of the sphere and influence a mother has is in the life of Sarah

Edwards, the wife of Jonathan Edwards, a minister and early colonist. Sarah raised 11 children while her husband busied himself with writing and ecclesiastical duties, becoming the famous one of the family. She stayed in the background as a homemaker —valuing each child's individuality and intelligence, educating both sons and daughters, but also teaching them to work responsibly. A genealogical study later tracked down 1,400 of the descendants and compared them to another family who were notorious for criminality and welfare dependency. The Jukes family cost the state of New York a total of $1,250,000 in welfare and custodial charges, while the Edwards descendants boasted the following: 13 college presidents, 65 professors, 100 lawyers and a dean of an outstanding law school, 30 judges, 66 physicians and a dean of a medical school, 80 holders of public office, 3 U.S. Senators, mayors of 3 large cities, governors of 3 states, a Vice President of the U.S. and a controller of the U.S. Treasury, not to mention the countless numbers who were successful in business and the arts. Only 2 of these 1,400 were "black sheep," which eloquently testifies to the power of one woman who wasn't afraid of a few diapers." (Elizabeth D. Dodds, *Marriage to a Difficult Man: The Uncommon Union of Sarah and Jonathan Edwards* [Philadelphia: Westminster Press, 1971], as quoted in Tamara Allred, *From Deadlines to Diapers*, p. 38.)

## The Refiner's Fire

I had an intriguing opportunity to go through a pottery factory several years ago. The pots—beautiful creations of many lovely earthen shades of clay, with graceful and varied shapes and curves—were interesting to see before they went to the firing process. In fact, they were so lovely as they were that I asked a craftsman nearby, whose hands were the same color as the pots, why they needed to be fired.

"Oh, dear," he replied, trying not to show his disdain for my ignorance, "if we didn't fire them, they would fall apart very quickly. The least bump, not to mention time itself, would simply crumble them away. The firing makes the pots strong and durable and so much more beautiful, inside and out." His eyes gleamed as he held up a fine example.

How true this is of motherhood! We start our mothering careers as rather ordinary-looking clay pots with varied shapes and curves, and march directly into the refiner's fire.

Of course, a fire can either give luster and depth and strength or it can burn and destroy. How well we use the heat is the key.

Lately I've had a chance to see several close friends whom I hadn't seen since high school or roommate days—before any of us had children. I see in them now, several children later, a special luster—something almost indescribable, but I know that it comes from the refiner's fire.

We can feel the fire making us more patient and understanding in spite of ourselves. We learn to handle impossible situations with a smile. We begin to understand the pure love of Christ as we love our husbands and children in spite of their "difficulties."

I sat in a women's meeting not long ago, enthralled with the things that were being said. The music was heavenly and the spoken word uplifting and inspiring. I felt my spirit climb to a higher realm and I was so proud and happy to be a woman, especially a mother. Tears welled up in my eyes and a lump in my throat as I realized the majesty of what I was struggling to become. I was thrilled by the voices and faces of a beautiful women's chorus as I watched the light in their eyes.

As I drove home alone that evening, I promised myself that I would stay in that higher realm. I felt real joy as I realized that the children were progressing, and I felt excited about some things I could do for all of us that would help to keep us in that realm.

That night, the baby woke up twice and our two-year-old wet the bed so thoroughly that the bedding had to be completely changed. Already tired when I got up the next morning, I faced the reality of a hectic schedule that included church meetings, car-pools, a guest for dinner, spelling homework with a child who never remembered, and a toothache. By late afternoon

I realized how easily that higher realm could be eclipsed by the mundane survival of the fittest.

We have to make very conscious decisions about *how* to remain in the higher realm, or dreams become disasters and life lives us instead of vice versa. The fire begins to destroy rather than refine. We must never lose sight of our dreams—even though we may reach them by way of a different path than we had expected. We can learn to expect the inevitable disasters and disappointments of daily living with children. Instead of letting them destroy us, we can learn to make them tools for a triumph next time around. B. H. Roberts said, "There is no progression from ease to ease."

The following chapters are designed to give specific how-tos and challenges to help you become a better mother. You must understand, however, that I do not claim that most of the ideas are mine. Many come from friends who are better mothers than I, and from a truly remarkable husband whose amazing practices outshine anything he may preach.

# Chapter Two

# *Keep Looking Upward*

*I* don't know how mothers survive without help from above—
especially when there are so many crucial dilemmas determining
which direction a person's life will take. The most comforting
thought I have is that somebody is really up there caring about
me (and you). It almost frightens me sometimes to realize that
the Lord is so close and ready to help in times of need. (It makes
me think that I really need to keep my life straight.) Oftentimes
the greatest challenge is accepting and agreeing with the answers
he provides.

I'd like to share with you, in the following story, one of the
greatest learning experiences of my life.

## Another Baby?

*The Reservation*

I could feel it coming on. The baby was getting around on
his own pretty well, and I felt wonderful. The other four children, although they had their individual ups and downs, were
basically secure and happy. The piano practicing was getting
more regular because I was able to be behind it a little more consistently. And with the baby just beginning to walk, I felt wings
of independence and a sense of joy in watching the children
grow and relate to the world around them. What worried me was
the nagging feeling in the back of my mind that it might be time
to have another baby.

I quickly remembered the many times I had said to myself
when the last baby was tiny, "Now, remember, remember,
*remember* how hard it is to have a new little baby! It takes all
your time and attention. You never get enough sleep because
you're up twice in the night with the baby, and then of course
there's no hope for a nap during the day with a two-year-old and
a four-year-old in the house, both ready to 'search and destroy'

at any moment. You're so tired that you're a grouch with your husband and children all the time. Besides, you have to be on duty every three or four hours—day and night—to nurse the baby, so that every outing, whether it be a fireside or grocery shopping, has to be scheduled to the minute.

"Waking every morning to the baby's cries cuts down on and sometimes eliminates your time with the scriptures and makes it much harder to have morning prayer. And it's like a never-ending race every morning to change and feed the baby while you supervise the practicing and settle an argument about who gets to sit by Daddy, before you organize the breakfast amidst pleas of 'Write my teacher a note' and 'Give me some lunch money.' Then you get to dress and then dress again the two-year-old who has been using the butter for play dough while you check to see that the beds are made and oversee the getting ready for school, complete with the perpetual last-minute scramble for Saren's toothbrush, Shawni's mittens, and Josh's shoes. Finally you struggle to get them out of the door with a smile pasted over your gritted teeth and a 'Have a nice day.' Next you try to help Saydi get her shirt on frontwards for nursery school while talking on the phone to someone with a problem, and then you have to fish the cat out of the toilet where Saydi has put him to try his luck.

"You just don't have time for another baby!" I told myself over and over, to help me remember how lovely the comparative peace of routine was becoming.

We, as a family, were just going into the third year of the greatest opportunity of our lives. My husband was president of the London South Mission, and we were having a marvelous experience—not without challenges, however, as the demands were great. Feeding mobs of missionaries, speaking at conferences, preparing our home for firesides for investigators and for new members who were struggling, and fixing dinners for everyone from stake presidents to General Authorities to members of Parliament kept me hopping.

Always before I had been thoroughly excited about the prospect of having a new spirit join our family. We had been married eight years and had five children: Saren, seven; Shawni, six; Josh, four; and Saydi, two and one-half, had come with us from America, and we had been blessed to have one child born in England—our little British boy, Jonah. My hesitation this time caused me to examine my own heart. Was I afraid after Jonah's difficult arrival? That was not it. Could it be that I simply did not want to give up my freedom to participate in all the activities of the mission? As I wrestled with the pros and cons (mostly cons) and with the deep, dark feeling I got every time I thought about another baby, my husband, who was feeling the same dilemma, suggested that on Sunday we should follow the same procedure that we had with the other children and have a special day of fasting and prayer to get an answer.

To be very honest, I did not even want to ask, because I was afraid of what the answer might be. However, I finally consented, with the thought in mind that maybe the answer this time *might* be, "No, not yet, take care of the responsibilities you have now and wait." *Oh, please tell me that!* I thought.

"Okay, Richard," I said in my most determined voice. "But we have *got* to have a very explicit answer and we'll have to fast forty-eight or even seventy-two hours, if necessary, to be absolutely sure." I saw him go a little pale around the mouth, because fasting is one of his hardest things. After a minute he patted me on the shoulder and said, "Let's start with twenty-four and see how it goes."

Sunday rolled around, and as we neared the end of our fast we compared our lists of pros and cons and started talking about them in earnest so that we could take a yes or no decision to the Lord for confirmation. About that time, however, the children began to get pretty noisy. Daddy called Saren, our oldest, over to the table.

"Would you please take your brothers and sisters up to the playroom and entertain them for an hour while Mom and Dad have a very serious talk, honey?" Curious about what we were doing, our very mature little seven-year-old demanded to know what was so important before she would consent.

"Well," he said after a moment of deliberation, "we're trying to decide whether or not to ask Heavenly Father to send a new little person to be in our family." She smiled wryly and happily herded the others up the stairs.

For what seemed like a very long time we worked on an extensive list of possibilities, and finally decided mutually, much to my chagrin, that it was time to have another baby if we could get a confirmation from the Lord and if he would grant us that privilege once again. As we knelt down, I remember having felt what I can only describe as black, dark, and numb. I just didn't know how I could possibly do it! I suppose I was hoping not for a confirmation but for a "stupor of thought" that would tell us to reconsider.

## The Revelation

Kneeling across from me and holding my hands, Richard began the prayer. The minute he said, "We have decided that now is the time to ask for another choice spirit, if that is thy will for us," I began to feel what I would describe as a bright light of peace settling over me, starting from the top of my head and spreading to every part, right down to my fingers and toes. It was as though the Lord was saying forcefully, in his own peaceful way: "It's all right, Linda. This baby is what you need; I've got a good one up here—one who needs to come now and who will teach you many things. I'll provide a way to get it all done. All is well. Be at peace."

By the time Richard's prayer was finished and I had offered mine, a conviction that a new person would join us and that all would be well was burning inside me, overwhelming, all-consuming, and undeniable. I was a new person, at perfect peace and ready for change. Most answers the Lord had given me were not nearly so dramatic—merely nudges in the right direction and good feelings. I was so gratified for this special, sure knowledge that he was there, loving and caring and answering.

While we were still holding hands and glowing in the aftermath of this beautiful spiritual experience, Saren, who could somehow sense that we were finished, came trotting into the dining room with a happy smile on her face and some pieces of paper in her hand.

"I organized the kids upstairs," she said. "I had them all sit in a circle on the floor and gave them each a piece of paper. Shawni and I wrote the names of the kids at the top of each paper. We told them to put a big check in the middle of the paper if they wanted a new baby brother or sister." She handed me five pieces of paper with five bold checkmarks below the names. It was now a unanimous family decision!

In the following few days, largely because of the good feelings I had about the answer the Lord had given me, I felt particularly close to him and my mind was flooded with things that were revelations to me. I had been going along these past seven years being a faithful, loving mother: having children, learning the hows and whens and wheres, but not really realizing the *whys!*

I projected myself ahead in time and tried to look at life and the childbearing years from an eternal perspective. I was startled to realize that in all eternity I would have only about twenty years in which to bear physical children on a physical earth and reap the eternal joys therein: the joy of learning to manage time and feelings and people, and the joy of molding lives and developing relationships that would help me to learn and grow forever. Only twenty years! Right now it seems like such a long time to change diapers and stand in foyers with fussy, noisy children, to prepare meals and put on bandages. Yet (as so many mothers just past the childbearing years tell me), soon there will be only a memory of how I did, to what extent I was anxiously engaged in grasping all the joy and happiness that was there for me to find in that short time. Then it will be over—forever!

I began to concentrate less on the difficulties of pregnancy and childbearing, on the complications of organizing life around an infant, on the heavy responsibility of having another person totally dependent on me. I began to see it all from a new perspective: My eyes were opened, and like a warm, wooly parachute settling over me, the whys began to make themselves manifest.

Having another child is a great blessing to be looked forward to with enthusiasm and excitement. I began to relish the change (the essence of the Savior's message: "You can change") and the challenges that would follow, to pour my energies into this real priority and to organize my life to do so, because the opportunity for that particular time in life only comes once and doesn't last very long. Children grow and change; so do situations; so do I. I began to relish the joy of balancing my life to make scrubbing floors and windows secondary to watching and relating to children and perceiving their needs before they became real problems.

I began to realize what a great blessing it is to struggle to teach a child the correct principles of life, and to make the home a great medium to do so. What we teach our children, how we mold their characters to try to make them responsible family members, loyal citizens, and noble children of God, affects not only us and them but their children and their children's children—an awesome and exciting challenge!

As the days passed I began to realize that my body was my most valuable earthly possession because of the miracles it could perform. If the condition that it was in was the determining factor in how many children I'd be privileged to have, I'd better take it a little more seriously. I felt an urgency to get in first-class physical condition so that I would be *able* to bear children as well as humanly possible for me. I decided that being in shape would alleviate the discomfort of the first few and last few months of the pregnancy, not to mention the benefits to the health of the baby. I had always known it made a difference, but I hadn't taken it seriously enough in the past to worry much about it. By "number six" with the hopes of more to come, it was serious business. I began a short crash course of physical fitness and realized that keeping fit between pregnancies was as important as during. The whole revelation was exhilarating.

The things that had worried me during past pregnancies seemed small and unimportant in light of the eternal perspective. Suddenly all the counsel given by the prophets came to life: "Have children unless there are health reasons involved. Put your family first; cut out the trivia, the excess, and concentrate on *them*. The rewards will be immediate *and* long-term . . . forever."

*The Resolution*

Those were the feelings that came to me in England. And our sixth child was even more of a blessing than the Lord had promised us. But that was months ago. How is it going today?

I often reflect on an experience which reconfirmed my feelings. I had to get to a certain department store to return two big bedspreads which I had taken for my mother to approve. Having decided that I would just have time to get them returned and still pick up my two oldest daughters at school within half an hour, I piled the other four children in the car (one of them without shoes, as it was midsummer and I simply didn't have any time to search).

In the store I discovered there was no elevator, so I quickly organized a plan for the escalator. Because they would not allow open strollers on the moving stairs, I folded mine up and hung it over my right arm. On the same arm I perched that sweet sixth baby—now a seven-month-old angel innocently sucking his fist, completely unaware of my dilemma.

In my left hand I had the large plastic garbage sack into which I had put the bedspreads to protect them from the peanut butter. In front of me were five-year-old Josh, studying the mechanics of the escalator, and two-year-old Jonah, fidgeting around with no shoes on his feet. Behind me was cute four-year-old Saydi in her self-chosen "orphan outfit," wearing jam from ear to ear, singing embarrassingly loud (thus destroying my efforts to remain unnoticed) and enjoying the ride.

As we approached the top, Josh got off with a grand gesture of accomplishment, but Jonah, bless his screeching little heart, panicked and bolted, having decided he was not getting off but was going back down. The scene that resulted was hysterical. Josh started yelling, "Hey, Mom, Jonah's stuck!" Jonah started screaming at the top of his lungs. I grabbed for him, thinking that surely his little toes were being mangled in the escalator's iron teeth. Saydi, who was helplessly being bashed into me from behind, was bellowing like a sick cow. Poor baby Talmadge was screaming with horror because, as I had lurched to grab Jonah, he had fallen backwards and was literally hanging upside-down by his knees on my arm.

Somehow I got everybody off that escalator with no fatalities, and I comforted the snuffly children and dried their tears. Completely hassled and upset at myself for being so stupid as to even try such a dumb thing, all I could think of was, *Linda, what are you doing with all these kids!*

I quickly tried to compose myself and hurry on, as I knew that my two grade-schoolers would be waiting. As luck would have it, I got behind two very slow little old ladies—one in rubber boots and the other in a little black pillbox hat with net flowing around the top. We were in a narrow aisle and simply could not get past. They had been near the "scene of the accident," but they were completely oblivious to my situation, even though there were still some whimpers and sniffles from the children.

Just at the point of exasperation, I couldn't help hearing one say to the other in a very loud but sweet little-old-lady voice, "Oh, no, Agnes, I don't want any yarn today; I've got enough yarn to last two years!"

That statement really sank in, and I stopped dead in my tracks and started to giggle about the whole situation. As I looked at those two little ladies picking through the yarn and then glanced back at my whimpering children, I got a flash of inspiration as the answer to my question. A feeling of sheer joy and gratitude for my children overwhelmed me. I *knew* what I was doing with all these kids, and I was so happy to be in my shoes instead of in the other ladies' "boots."

Inevitably we all get into some dire situations at times, and for my part I find it helps to lighten the load if I can look at them with a little humor, as I was able to on this occasion. This helps me to put things in perspective, too, and particularly to reinforce my sense of appreciation.

Please do not misunderstand what I am saying. I am certainly not advocating that all parents should have lots of children. I am merely trying to share the exhilarating feeling of knowing that as wives and mothers, husbands and fathers, we are entitled to personal revelation, especially when it concerns our own or our children's lives. This is true whether our children number one or ten, and whether the Lord sends them to us through natural means or adoption. This is a glorious knowledge.

When times are hard (and certainly there are times of real trial, not just momentary desperation), I remember that sure, sweet answer that my Heavenly Father gave me that assured us we were to have that sixth child. It scares me to think of the resentments and doubts I might have felt if I had just gone ahead having new babies without that calm, peaceful assurance from the Lord.

## Life Is Fragile—Handle With Prayer

As pointed out previously, prayer is the key to many things. It can give us peace and calmness of heart and mind. It helps us to make hard decisions, especially if we make our own decision first and then take it to the Lord for a confirmation—rather than expect him to make the decision for us.

Prayer can help us resolve dilemmas and overcome bad feelings toward others, and can guide us in our relationships with husbands and children. The Lord has told us over and over in the scriptures that he is anxious to help us if we will but ask!

I was struck with the beauty and meaning of an original oil painting in one of the cathedrals we visited in England. It was the often-reprinted painting of the Savior, standing in his glorious light, knocking at the door. As I viewed the original painting, I noticed for the first time that there was no doorknob on his side. The person on the other side had to open the door in order to see the light.

Sometimes, we as mothers have experiences that give us glimpses into the feelings of the Savior as expressed in this painting. I had one such experience on a Sunday morning—Mother's Day, in fact—when I realized as I was running the bath water for my two- and three-year-olds that they needed to practice some songs for the Mother's Day program later that morning. The song book, however, had been left in the car the night before.

*I'll just quickly slip out to the garage and get it,* I thought as I scampered across the kitchen, still in my old white nightgown, and closed the door behind me to keep the house warm. I could hear our fifteen-month-old baby boy, who had followed me as far as the door, complaining about being left in and fiddling with the doorknob as I rummaged through the car for the song book. After a couple of minutes of searching through suitcases, dirty clothes, and styrofoam hamburger boxes, I laid my hands on the song book and went running back to the door, only to bash my nose as my momentum was stopped with a bang.

With horror, I realized that the baby's fascination for pushing buttons had carried through to the doorknob, and I was locked out. I could hear him still shuffling around in the hall, but no matter what I said, he just couldn't figure out how to turn that knob without at least one lesson from someone on the same side of the door.

Dying at the thought of running around our well-exposed house in my "lovely" nightgown, I'd almost decided to try to communicate through the closed door until Daddy got home from his meeting in about half an hour, when I remembered that I had left our two little girls in the bathtub—with the water running.

Swallowing a big lump of pride, I took a big breath and tiptoed swiftly out of the garage door, around the house, onto the balcony, and to the bathroom window (which had the kind of frosted glass you can't see through) where I could hear the water running full blast and the children's voices.

"Saren," I called gingerly to our oldest daughter (the three-year-old), trying not to speak loud enough to call any attention to my presence from the neighbors. No response. The running water was too loud. "Saren," I yelled, louder and louder until it reached an almost scream. At last she recognized my voice.

"Mommy!" she shouted, "it's getting hot!" I knew she didn't know how to work the knobs on the tub. In horror all I could think to say was, "Get out of the tub."

"I can't hear you," she kept saying through the thick, frosted window.

Casting all modesty to the wind, I yelled louder and louder:

"Get out of the tub. *Get out of the tub!* GET—OUT—OF—THE
—TUB!"

I could feel the neighbors' kitchen curtains parting behind
me but I didn't dare look around and wave. I just clutched my
nightgown, which the breeze was whipping around me, a little
tighter and started yelling, "*Come and open the balcony door.*"

After several more "I can't hear you"s from Saren and
screams on my part I finally heard her padding to the sliding
glass door. I had heard two-year-old Shawni giggling about all
the commotion, so I knew she wasn't in distress—yet. Only a few
more seconds and I would be able to pull her out of the rising
water.

As Saren reached the door in her birthday suit, dripping
from head to toe, I began to explain how to open the door and
realized that my trial was not yet over. That door was almost
always unlocked; she had never tried to open the lock on it
before. Pushing the lever in the right spot was a fairly complex
maneuver for a three-year-old.

I tried to remain calm, and explained over and over just how
to open the door. After what seemed like an eternity, she at last
hit the right spot and in a flash the door was wide open. I threw
my arms around Saren on my way into the bathroom, where we
found Shawni shoulder deep in water, enjoying her toy boat at
almost nose level, with the water pouring down the overflow
valve. The baby toddled in to see what all the commotion was
and we all just giggled with relief.


The feelings of that morning flooded back to me as I gazed at
that picture of the Savior standing with his light at the door
with no handle. How desperately he must want to get in and
help us avoid the dangers of life, if we would only open the door.
Until we do, he is helpless because he will not force his will upon
us.

Prayer is a vital way for us to ask for guidance and help and
to offer thanks and love. It is also a beautiful way to help our
children realize how much we love and care for them and how
totally we trust in a loving Heavenly Father for their welfare.

I once heard Mrs. Norman Vincent Peale speak on the subject of bringing spirituality into our homes. She related a very touching practice from her own home. She said that ever since her children had been old enough to be away from her, on special days she would say to them, "What time is your field trip?" or, "What time is your test?" They knew she asked those questions so that she could pray for them at those precise times. Several incidents were cited wherein those prayers had been answered. "Now," she said, "when I go to make a speech or to fulfill a special assignment, my children say to me, 'Mom, what time is your talk?'"

To me it seems that prayer is more important to a young mother than almost any other single thing. The scriptures admonish us to pray always, and, even more specifically, to pray morning, noon, and night (Alma 34:21).

I once asked a young mother to pray three times a day for one week and then to report to a women's group the following Sunday on what difference it made. She was full of enthusiasm when she reported. She said she had been so much more calm and understanding with her children—able to give music instruction without confrontation. "Our home was a much happier place to live in!" she said. Then, almost as an afterthought, she added: "It's one of the hardest things I've ever had to do—to find time to talk to the Lord amidst daily demands. Boy, am I glad that week is over!"

Mothers would all admit that it is really hard to find time to pray—especially when you're awakened by the baby crying, or by your three-year-old Annie-look-alike singing from her room, "Please won't you come get your baby—maybe?" Sometimes the only way is to pray while you are doing the dishes, or to offer a quick prayer requesting needed strength and endurance just before the kids get home from school.

Not only is praying on your own and with your husband vital, but also praying with the children, collectively and individually. It seems we often agonize with a child about a problem at school or with friends, and then finally, as a last resort, pray about it and receive an immediate answer. My typical reaction is, "Now, why didn't I think of that in the first place!"

Some of the happiest experiences in our family revolve around prayers that were answered: from the prayer of a lost child to find his way home to prayers for sick brothers and sisters or pets.

Prayer can improve our attitudes, expand our understanding, enlarge our capacity to endure, and inspire our minds—if we will only let it.

## Use Your Handbook: The Scriptures

Many of you good mothers have a natural affinity for reading the scriptures. You read them every day—or almost every day—just out of sheer desire to feel their strong influence in your lives.

I'm sorry to say that I am not always one of you. I have gone through several years during which I read intensely, and then again several months when I thought about the scriptures much more than I read them. At other times I am only reminded of them on Sunday when I realize I have forgotten to bring my scriptures to the services.

As I analyzed this situation, I found something interesting. There were two particular sets of circumstances in my life as a mother during which I was diligent about reading the scriptures: (1) when I was having personal problems or there was a major crisis in our family, and (2) when I had firmly committed myself to read a certain number of pages within a certain amount of time.

The first method takes care of itself and has marvelous effects. I remember specifically struggling to understand faith as our fifth child, born nine weeks early, lay in an intensive-care unit with a 50 percent chance of living, and when my own life hung in the balance. Those scriptures almost popped off the page at me in the aftermath of unexpected hemorrhage and emergency delivery. They gave me hope and a perfect faith that that little child would be a normal, healthy, and special person.

When things are going well, however, what we feel toward the scriptures amidst our hectic lives is often guilt—because we're not reading them more regularly.

In thinking over my study of the scriptures, I realize that the first time I made it through an entire volume of scripture—cover to cover, in order—was when I had been meeting with other mothers. We had committed to each other to read a certain number of pages by a certain time, and to check on each other until we had all finished.

The pressure was on, and I read. It was wonderful; I found so many treasures that I had never noticed before. Since then, when I have reread the scriptures, I have realized that the word of the Lord is really like a beautiful kaleidoscope. As you look into the scriptures there is always a beautiful new design, with intricate patterns that mean something different each time you read the words. Because you are a different person, you understand them on a different level each time you read. Often different things stand out because of particular experiences you are having at that point in life.

The scriptures are beautiful. I have never sat down to read them, even for ten minutes, without finding something that applied to me—that day! They keep our minds soaring and our thoughts in a higher realm.

Many study classes and scripture marathons have come and gone, but the key I have found most useful is indicated in the following lines:

| If a person: | His chance of actually doing it is: |
|---|---|
| 1. Hears a good idea | 20 percent |
| 2. Plans *how* to do it | 40 percent |
| 3. Decides *when* to do it | 55 percent |
| 4. Discusses it with another person— tells that person he will do it | 80 percent |
| 5. Sets a future meeting where the other person will ask him if he did it | 95 percent |

Although our mothers' group didn't know about this study, our plans to read the scriptures certainly validated it.

Recently Allison, a friend of our twelve-year-old Saren, came up with a plan originally designed by Ardeth Kapp, a great champion for youth. Basically, it was a plan wherein the girls decided to read a certain set of scriptures by a certain date. It involved reading only two and one-half pages per night or sixteen pages per week. The girls were to check up on each other each Sunday to make sure that the quota for the week was reached.

Getting in on the fun, I agreed with Saren to read the scriptures with her each day and follow the same guidelines. The result was exciting. Though we had read the scriptures often as a family, I had not read much with the children one on one. It was a truly joyful experience! I felt true rapture as I saw the scriptures come alive in that child's mind when we read aloud each night. I was amazed to find that she understood more on the first reading than I had on the fifth.

Sometimes, when the schedule won't allow us to read together, we read separately and then compare notes weekly. It is an exciting experience—all because we're motivated! (We know we're going to get that phone call on Sunday.) Sometimes we may miss several days and then scramble to catch up, but as long as we're on the right page by Sunday, at least we have met the deadline. (Of course, it's better to read the scriptures on a daily basis.) Best of all, we are edified and inspired by the word of the Lord through his prophets.

Sometimes, after you have a feeling for the flow of events in the scriptures, it's very interesting to allot a certain amount of time every day for reading rather than to try to get through a certain number of pages or chapters. The riches of the scriptures make it exciting to occasionally spend the whole fifteen minutes or half-hour on one page, or even on one or two special verses.

It is also important, I think, to let your children see you reading your scriptures just for yourself. Try getting up a few minutes before the kids (if possible) and let them find you reading the scriptures when they trundle in with bleary eyes. Or try setting your scripture-reading time a half an hour before the older children return from school (maybe while the baby sleeps). Let them find you reading the scriptures when they bounce in from school. It's bound to improve the after-school spirit of your home.

I once heard an amusing story about "The Notorious Cold Bath Mother." A young mother with four adopted children under four said that she had finally decided that the only place she could stay awake while reading the scriptures was in a cold bath. (Some people will do anything.)

There are many interesting things to read beckoning to us each day, from newspapers and magazines to recipe books and Church books. Yet we will be happier if we can remember to put the scriptures first—even though there is often no time to read anything else. (If you haven't read the scriptures today, put this book down and do it now.)

---

## Share Spiritual Experiences

"Do our children have spiritual experiences every week?" Richard and I wondered one Sunday night when we were talking about the children's strengths and weaknesses. We knew there were special occasions when they had felt spiritual help, such as when they had gotten lost and prayed to find their way. "How often do they feel that special help?" we wondered. We planned to find out.

The next Sunday, after the hubbub of trying to get everybody settled at the table for dinner, when things were reasonably quiet, Daddy announced: "All right, children, tonight we want you all to think hard about a spiritual experience you've had this past week and share it with the family. We'll give you a minute to think and then we'll start with Saren."

Things quieted almost to a hush, and then the almost unanimous reaction was, "I haven't had a spiritual experience this week!"

"Now, wait a minute and let me explain what we mean by a spiritual experience," I encouraged. "Sometimes it's something big like a sick child praying to be healed and being given health, but most of the time it comes in simple little ways—like feeling good about sharing a toy or helping me clean when you know I'm really tired. That warm feeling in your heart is the Holy Ghost telling you that you've done the right thing. Sometimes it's just praying for a little help with a problem and receiving a quick, sure feeling. Now think again."

One by one the children saw the light. One child recalled that she had lost her math homework and prayed desperately to find it. She had been led to an old folder where she had absent-mindedly filed it. "I know Heavenly Father helped me!" she beamed.

Three of the older children remembered that they had prayed really hard for our little dog when she had had a brief seizure the day before. (Maybe she would have recovered anyway, but I discovered long ago that the faith of a child can work miracles.) Each reported having had a warm feeling that the pup would be okay.

Each little child thought of a special warm feeling he or she had experienced that week, right down to the five-year-old who said, "It makes me feel happy when I say 'I love you'," and the three-year-old who said, "The other day ago I woke up in my bed and you were gone and I thought you were 'died,' but then I remembered you were at the restaurant and I felt happy."

Now every Sunday, during our Sunday meal, we discuss briefly what each child learned in his or her Sunday School class and then have each report on a spiritual experience from that week. Dad and Mom report, too! It's amazing to realize that, had we not taken a moment to think about them, those precious moments might have been forgotten and left unappreciated. This discussion gives the children a chance to consciously realize that they are being helped and guided from above. More importantly, it makes them aware of their opportunities to ask for spiritual help during the week ahead.

CHALLENGES

This chapter ends with four challenges. Don't try to do them all at once, but do plan to do them. Write down a definite time and place to get them accomplished.

1. Pray morning, noon, and night for one week—about specifics. Include the Lord in more of your thoughts and decisions. You'll be amazed at how much help he is ready to give if you just ask. On the big decisions, make your own judgment first and then go to the Lord for a confirmation. He'll give you a definite good feeling if the answer is "yes," or a stupor of thought or cold, confused feeling if you need to redecide.

How can you remember to pray? Try wearing your watch backwards on your wrist so that every time you look at it, it will remind you. Have family prayer morning and evening with all the family involved for one week. Give special attention to gratitude and thanksgiving.

2. Tell a child that you will be praying for him at a time when he needs special help. If you have special needs, ask him to pray for you, too.

3. Read the scriptures every day for a predetermined amount of time. Read them (1) individually, (2) with your husband, (3) with your children, (4) with a friend, or (5) any combination or all of the above. Try memorizing one verse per week with your family. Decide on a program (time, place, method), and tell someone that you're going to do it and that you want to be checked on by a certain date. Then *do it!*

4. Have your children verbalize a spiritual experience around the dinner table or at a family home evening or devotional once a week.

You'll be amazed at how much these four simple things will help you to keep looking upward.

# Chapter Three

# Reduce Stress—Increase Joy

Most of us start out our careers as mothers thinking we are going to be the world's best: always kind, patient, and understanding, always having hot cookies waiting for hungry mouths after school.

One of my favorite book titles describes exactly my feelings at the end of a hard day: *I Didn't Plan to Be a Witch!* When many little mouths and hands need many things at the same time, I have a "crumple point" at which I lose all patience and understanding and become a wicked witch with a wart on my nose.

I spoke to a mother one day who was so tied up with the stress of dealing with the demands of her children, caring for their needs, settling squabbles, and resolving problems that she said she was beginning to cringe every time she heard someone yell "Mom!" "I can't stand it," she went on. "Every time I hear someone yell that word I feel I'd like to scream."

We all know what this mother means, but we also know that the tension that builds up in us can affect the whole family negatively. Everyone gets upset and irritable if the mother is tense and grouchy. It may not seem fair, but it's true that the parents set the tone in a home, and the mother is the kingpin.

Whenever I can, I try to calm my mind by thinking that our attitude and behavior affect everyone we contact; and that, since life consists mainly of small events and common circumstances, the best way I can contribute is to be as peaceful, as kind, and as cheerful as possible in my everyday life, especially in my interactions with my family.

If only we could think such thoughts every morning before diving into our daily adventures! Giving those everyday moments peace and pleasantness is probably our greatest challenge.

Hard as motherhood is, there are many clear ways to cut down on the inevitable stress and strain to the mother in a busy household. If you get to the end of this book and feel as if you've tried everything and still come to those moments when you feel like throwing in the towel, remember the solution for stress attributed to Theodore Roosevelt: "When you get to the end of your rope—tie a knot and hang on!"

When it comes to coping with stress, mothers can't just sit by and hope things get better. We must *plan* not to be witches. It is essential for survival! The following ten sections, five in this chapter and five in chapter 4, point out several keys that can make the most disastrous days seem almost humorous, the hard times bearable, and the joyful times unforgettable. The challenges at the end of each section are designed to help you to formulate and execute some of your own plans for relief.

---

## 1. Remain Calm in the Face of Adversity

### Analyze Your Situation

Sit down for a while after a particularly hectic (but typical) day and try to analyze what happened. I did this one day when, after a wild morning, Richard sent me away to write. The following story tells, as I recorded it in my journal, what happened that day. (This is an absolutely true account. Nothing has been added or deleted.)

#### Morning Madness

We awoke at 6:00 A.M. to hear the baby sounding very hungry in his bed and the new puppies yipping to get out of their box downstairs. Both baby and animals had awakened us several times in the night and we could think of nothing that we would like more than to turn over and shut out the world for another hour.

After listening to the complaints for a few minutes, Daddy voluntarily decided that it was his turn to get the bottle. He dutifully picked up the baby and brought the big, soggy lump in to me while he went in search of the bottle.

In the meantime, "Miss Lark" Shawni, who is always the first child up, popped through the door and jumped onto the bed. We talked for a minute about whether or not Saren was up and then pulled ourselves out of bed and with determination plunged into the adventure of the day.

With Shawni's piano and Daddy's cello practicing as background music, Josh greeted me in the hall with a whining, disappointed voice. "Mom, the tooth fairy didn't come yet!"

Struck with guilt and horror at forgetting again, I tried to disguise my shame and said calmly, "Now, Josh, you know she's late sometimes. I'll bet she'll be here by seven o'clock."

Just then I noticed that Shawni was blundering her way through her Suzuki piano lesson in entirely the wrong way. I sat the soggy baby down in the hall to run and quickly correct her before it became a bad habit. I tried to be loving and positive and gently reminded her to find her book first instead of just trying to remember the piece.

By then Saren was behind me, after having been awakened and prodded by at least three different people to get out of bed. She was a half-hour late to start her practicing and had to interrupt Shawni by asking her to stand up so that she could find her violin shoulder pad in the piano bench. After several minutes of searching without luck, I told her in an exasperated voice to use mine, then dashed off to find Josh.

"Josh," I yelled down the stairs, "put on your shoes and come and do the orange juice. It's getting late!" As he started to the stairs, I vowed to get the tooth money under his pillow right then.

That same second there was a roar from a usually calm Daddy. The afterward muttering and sputtering told me that Shawni had forgotten to put out the dog and Daddy had stepped in the mess with his bare feet.

As I viewed the fiasco, I realized that five-year-old Saydi was banging on my leg, and I finally noticed that she was asking something over and over. I turned my mind in her direction (with soggy baby underfoot) and realized she was yelling over piano, violin, and Daddy's moans, "Where are the paper plates?" It was her job to set the table, and she knew I'd just bought paper plates at the store.

My eyes flashed around the kitchen a couple of times, and as I grabbed out the pancake griddle and started it heating I considered how nice it would be not to have to do dishes. But I couldn't see the paper plates. I directed Saydi to use regular plates. By this time Shawni was sawing away on her violin, completely oblivious to intonation, with her wrist tucked in the wrong way. Daddy had ignored my pleas for him to go in his den to practice and was playing his cello right next to us in the family room. He was playing "Tomorrow" by ear while Saydi gleefully sang along, occasionally waiting for him to find the right note.

Josh, who was working on the orange juice, was poking at it with a spoon and using his whining voice to say, "Maaam, you said I only had to do this job until last February and I'm still doing it!"

"Oh, we just decided that you were so good at it that you should keep doing it! Try to remember to take it out of the freezer the night before and it'll be a lot easier." (*At least he has his shoes,* I thought.)

"But, Maaaam," he said, "the tooth fairy still hasn't come!" Just then the soggy baby decided that he was going to demand to be picked up, and little Talmadge, who had fallen asleep in his clothes the night before, was hanging on my leg and saying, "My —pants—are—wet!" I could see that time was getting short— we were down to fifteen minutes for the prayer, scripture, break- fast, and three hair fix-ups before the big kids had to be out of the door to catch the bus. I threw the soggy baby in the high chair and took an unbelievably wet diaper off of two-year-old Talmadge. I decided to give him a few minutes to "air out" while I made breakfast before I put another diaper on him.

Shawni was by now playing her violin on a stool in the middle of the kitchen so I could help her while I got breakfast ready. Talmadge hung on my leg and cried because he was starving. I tried to get Shawni to straighten out her wrist and play her second finger a little higher. That was the fatal mistake. I forgot to praise her first! No matter what I said afterward about how good she was, she could not be consoled. She began to whine and wail about how she was trying her very best and thought she was "doing so good" and I just yelled at her.

After about three minutes of her nonstop whining, Daddy

called Shawni and me into the family room and told Shawni how important it was to quit whining. With reprimanded Shawni, soggy baby, and hungry Talmadge wailing in the background, I just lost it all and got good and mad at Josh for taking five minutes to find a knife to cut the butter in half with (so that we could have a chunk at each end of the table for the pancakes). I yelled at everybody to *kneel down*, threw on the pancakes, dumped the orange juice into a pitcher from the blender, tossed two squeeze bottles of syrup on the table, and threw the baby a cold pancake to play with while we had our prayer. After the prayer we all sat around the table long enough for Daddy to say, "I think we should all get back to our old idea of *whispering* in the mornings so that we can all feel the Holy Ghost."

Not meaning any disrespect to the Holy Ghost, I pasted on a smile and threw a few daggers at Daddy with my eyes, realizing that he had no idea either of what I had just been through or of how ridiculous that idea sounded just then. I finally decided that the moment had arrived when I really *had* to change the baby. I jumped up from the table, told Saren to take care of the pancakes, grabbed the poor, soggy, messy baby, ran in to change him and coo at him for one minute, and ran back out just in time to brush through Josh's hair and find my purse and divide up the lunch money. I passed the brush around to the girls who quickly picked up their things and dashed out the door. "Have a good day," I yelled as they ran for the bus. Josh was still looking for his spelling book, but after deciding that it wasn't to be found, he decided to leave without it. As he dashed for his coat he said, "Mom, the tooth fairy never did come."

I grabbed at my throat and, in a completely disgusted voice, said, "That dumb fairy! She's always so late! I'm sure she'll have it taken care of by the time you get home from school." I kissed him on the head and said, "Now run, you'll be late for the bus!" Consoled, he obliged.

I walked back into the kitchen to see bleary-eyed, four-year-old Jonah, who had slept through the whole thing, come padding in and say, "I'm hungry. I want pancakes right now."

At that moment I realized that I had let Talmadge "air out" too long. He was standing on the window seat, watching a bird in the bird feeder, and was obliviously more interested in the bird than the potty.

I quickly cleaned up the puddle, flopped the baby down with a bottle, and hurried up the pancakes for Jonah while I sewed the hem on afternoon-kindergartner Saydi's skirt (which had been "hanging" the last three times she'd worn it), then dashed downstairs to see if I could find the little urchin some socks— her most diminished commodity.

As I hurried to get *myself* ready, Rick said: "Now, dear, if I'm going to baby sit for you like this you've just *got* to get out of here sooner." Wincing a little, but realizing again that he couldn't have known what I'd just been through, I was grateful to be leaving—with or without prodding.

So here I am—writing at last—thinking how often scenes like this occur at our house, and feeling a little anxious to get home and put some money under Josh's pillow.

I hope everybody can identify with some parts of a morning like the one I've just described.

After reading this incident over several times, I discovered several things that could have cut down considerably on the hassle. I found that with a couple of training sessions our six- and seven-year-olds could fix breakfast. In fact, they loved making breakfast and learned to fix scrambled eggs, pancakes, and waffles as well as dry and cooked cereal. While they cooked, I worked with the older children on music. One of the "big kids" changed the baby while I got myself ready for action. I could see that I could change many unnecessary little irritations, while others were unpredictable and had to be coped with in a certain frame of mind. To make a long story short: Things got better.

## Expect a Few Disasters

Another of my favorite book titles is *The Majesty of Calmness*. There is something not only majestic but magical about remaining calm. It's easy to remain calm when there is no adversity. The hard thing is remaining calm when your two-year-old has a temper tantrum because you pulled him off the cupboard, the six- and eight-year-olds are arguing about whose turn it is to use the new toy, the ten-year-old is begging to sleep over with a friend, the four-year-old drops a dozen eggs on the floor, the doorbell is ringing, and your husband is waiting to talk to you on the phone.

This is not an unusual situation, as many of you know. This kind of thing happens several times a day. In all seriousness, I've decided that much exasperation is alleviated if I just expect several disasters every day. If nothing else, this eliminates the element of surprise. Sometimes it even adds to the excitement—keeping me wondering what will happen next.

## Decide on Calmness in Advance

I have worked on the concept of calmness harder than any other single thing because it is so hard for me. I am not basically a calm person. I have to plan not to be a witch.

One of the most helpful things to me in my struggle to remain calm is my learning to decide in advance. By that I mean that before I step out the door to "hit the action" every morning, I pray hard that I can keep a sweet, calm spirit in our home that day through the things I do or say. I think through, in the two minutes it takes me to brush my teeth or comb my hair, what I am going to do *when* (not if) the crisis arrives—even what I will say and how I will react. I am amazed, when I am consistent about doing this, how much difference it makes. When I get to the crunch I can (sometimes) think for a moment and remember what to do rather than lose control and have a temper tantrum.

I decide that I am going to remain the calm center of the hurricane—the eye of the storm, so to speak—the part that remains still when everything else is swirling around in disarray.

"Overpower them with calmness," my husband always says. Though I appreciate the advice, I think he sometimes is asking for the superhuman. However, it really helps to pull that thought to the surface when I feel my anger rising and about to pop out my ears in the form of smoke.

Another way to decide in advance is to spend time on Sunday thinking over the things that are upsetting in your household. When you've sorted through the general things, think of irritations caused by each child. As much as they love him, most parents can think of at least one thing that is a source of contention with each child. Methodically think through each of these sore spots and decide what you're going to do about them.

For example, one child may be whining every night at dinner time when everyone is hungry and tired anyway. Instead of becoming upset and taking it out on the other children, decide you will send him to his room until he is ready to quit whining.

Use your time in your Sunday Session (section 2 of this chapter) to actually make a chart something like the accompanying one.

| Child | Problem | My Reaction | My Plan for Better Action |
|---|---|---|---|
| Jimmy | Won't mind first time | Total exasperation and often anger | Establish special reward for minding without being reminded. |
| Janie | *Always* has little aches and pains | I give her the feeling that I don't want to hear about it and don't believe her. | Grit your teeth and show *real* sympathy. |
| John | Won't get up | I yell down the stairs for him to "get up" so many times that I get blue in the face and furious. | Give him his own alarm clock and let him be late a few times. Let *him* take consequences. |
| Angie | Worries about ridiculous things and won't be consoled. | I expect her to accept my "easy" solution, and then get caught up in an argument when she won't agree. | Treat worries seriously. Offer alternate solutions, then change the subject. Don't be enticed to argue. |

Use the principles of deciding in advance particularly at those predictable high-tension times in the day. In our home those times are in the early morning before school and when the children get home from school. Concentrate on ways to make those times smoother.

It took me many years to figure out how important those after-school hours are to making the rest of the day run smoothly. It is so easy to "upset the apple cart" if the mother is worried about preparing dinner or constantly running errands or car-pools during those hours.

I try to prepare dinner in the morning or early afternoon while the baby sleeps, and to cut down to an absolute minimum the after-school car-pool hours so that I can spend that time talking to the kids about their day or helping with homework.

Another approach is that of a friend who says that she likes to use those after-school hours just to play with her kids, or to provide some physical or emotional outlet for them until after dinner, when homework hour begins promptly at 7:00 P.M.

You have to plan according to your own family needs, but it's important to remember how crucial those after-school hours are. They can so easily slip into angry episodes because of pressures on mother and children.

Don't fall in step with the brigade of mothers who form a habit of running errands as soon as older children get home from school, so that the older kids can baby sit and Mom doesn't have to drag the preschoolers to the grocery store or the dry cleaners. Though I know sometimes this is absolutely necessary—especially to get other children to lessons and rehearsals—don't let yourself march along with the mothers whose children answer the phone every day after school and report that they don't know where their mother is or when she'll be back. Try to cut it to a minimum.

Those after-school hours can be the most productive hours of the day or the most disastrous—depending on your pre-determination.

My sister and I have gone through periods when we've had some fun with before- and after-school hours. We decided in advance how we were going to react to situations that arose, and then we were going to exude a certain aura and maintain it in those high-tension hours. Every school morning for two weeks we called each other to ask for a report on how well we had stuck to the goal. (It was fun, and the after-school hours got to be lots more fun too!)

One potential danger: It is possible to use calmness as an excuse for being inconsistent. We can't become so calm that we can watch with a smile as one child beats up on another, or as two little girls set up a birthday party for their dolls on the new couch, with graham crackers gobbed with sticky frosting and with grape juice to sip. We can't dismiss everything with a shrug and an "oh, never mind—they're having fun." We can't compromise principles or give up consistent discipline in the name of calmness.

## Two Solutions

In analyzing situations, Richard and I have decided that when we reach a breaking point in our dealing with the children, the best solution is to do one of two things: (1) force ourselves to become more calm, to swallow the anger, or (2) laugh. Some of the most dire situations, if viewed from another perspective, are hilarious.

One night at bedtime I remember clearly being absolutely furious with our four-year-old, who had pushed me to the absolute edge. I grabbed him by the shoulders and started to shake him and scold him vehemently. Suddenly he looked in my face and let out a peal of laughter. That made me even more angry, to think he would laugh in the face of such wrath, and I shook harder. Another peal of laughter. Finally I blared out, "What *are* you laughing about?!"

"Mommy, you look so funny," he roared. And his little brother in the other bed, who had been looking on with unbelief, started to laugh too. I thought for a minute about how ridiculous I must look, and then (though I tried not to) I broke up, too. Soon the other children heard us laughing and came running in to find out why. None of us could even explain. We just laughed until our sides hurt.

*Quarreling*

One of the most universal reasons for lack of calmness, on the part of both child and parent, is bickering or arguing. It can drive you up the wall sooner than any other single thing.

I smiled when a "model" mother of seven (herself the oldest of ten children) told us that she has to keep assuring her husband (an only child) that "all that quarreling" is normal. She says, "He just keeps saying, 'Are you sure this is normal?'"

Another mother mentioned a family that she knew in which the children were simply not allowed to argue in the home. One of the children in this family was telling her what a frustrated childhood she had had. It was very hard and sometimes damaging for her to live with pent-up feelings of anger.

On one occasion, while we were living in England, we had staying with us an official of the Church who was also the father of a large family. One day we asked, "How worried should we be about having such argumentative, strong-willed children who all think they have to have their own way?"

He looked back at us with a little twinkle in his eye and said, "If you're going to raise leaders, you've got to expect them to have and to be able to express their own opinions."

Even though that has comforted me many times, the fact remains that the right spirit cannot dwell in a home that is filled with arguing and bickering.

Once again, each mother needs to analyze her own system. Sometimes, to get responsibilities, chores, or practicing done, an elaborate chart may be required. Sometimes a system of rewards and punishments is necessary.

I still remember one occasion, at the beginning of a long trip (well, three hours) with nine bodies in the van, when Richard offered a visit to the favorite five-and-dime store when we reached our destination if *nobody* bickered. Lo and behold—it worked! We realized that it is possible!

The principle of repentance has worked very well to clear the air after a clash of feelings in our home. We require the perpetrator to say: "I'm sorry I hurt you. I won't do it again. Will you forgive me?" After a response from the injured—which for some reason has always been "yes"—they exchange a little hug and it's forgotten. The children know that repenting is the only way they can avoid punishment for having broken the "quarreling law."

Another good idea, suggested by a friend, is to send the two quarreling children each to an assigned "bench" separate from each other until each can decide what *he* did wrong. When each has done this, and only then, they can return and report to Mom or Dad. Presto—self-help!

In thinking hard about calmness one week, I passed through a series of scriptures that described the Savior's voice: a still voice of perfect mildness. What a wonderful way to describe the ideal! We can teach almost anything if we use the proper tone of voice.

In conclusion, let me reiterate that acquiring consistent calmness is not easy. For most people it is the hardest mental effort they will ever perform. But remember the eagle. When most birds fly away from a storm, the eagle will fly directly into the clouds and be lifted above the turbulence.

CHALLENGES

1. Analyze your situation and come up with your own solutions. Decide what you will do about the things that really bother you that you can change, and how you will handle the things that you can't.

This takes time and mental energy, but it is a great investment toward peace and harmony in the home, not to mention your own state of mind. Use some of the ideas in the next section to put solutions to work.

2. Learn to decide in advance. Each morning, use the time or make the time before you "hit the troops" to think through the kind of spirit you want to have prevail in your home. Go through things you might say or do in crisis or tense situations. In essence, program your mind to remain calm.

3. Spend a little time on Sunday sorting out and deciding in advance what to do about annoying idiosyncrasies of your children. Then stick to your plan!

4. Pinpoint high-tension times during the day and come up with a plan to alleviate the sources of irritation. Ask a relative or friend (or husband) to help you keep the plan foremost in your mind.

5. Keep the ideal in mind: a still voice of perfect mildness.

---

## 2. Sharpen Your Saw

When was the last time you felt as if for every step forward you were taking a couple backward? Whether it's keeping up with the dirty dishes in the sink or the mountains of laundry always needing to be done, it seems as though that feeling creeps in almost every day.

Often we become discouraged because we feel that our relationships aren't quite right with our husbands or children, and that there are more things to do than there are hours in the day. Sometimes we'd like to throw our arms in the air and quit, but the mouths are still there to feed and the telephone keeps ringing and we just keep plugging along—sawing away with a dull saw.

My husband's grandfather was a master carpenter. As a little boy, he used to watch his grandfather work, and he noticed that after cutting a few boards Grandpa's saw went slower and slower until smoke curled from the cutting edge and perspiration dripped from the old man's brow. The boy knew that even though his grandpa was anxious to finish the item or had a deadline for completion, he still took the time to sit on a stool and methodically sharpen the saw. Richard loved watching Grandpa's look of pleasure when he put the saw back to the board and it cut like a hot knife through butter.

So are we with our everyday lives. We can expend endless hours sawing away on things that seem important—running carpools and volunteering for the cancer drive and standing over kids while they practice—without spending a little concentrated, well-directed time "sharpening our saws."

One of the keys to survival as a mother is to have a set time and place wherein you can spend one hour a week completely alone and uninterrupted. We believe that the very best day for this is Sunday—a time to rest and re-create and plan for a successful week. (I say "we" because this was a system taught to me by my husband before we were married, and I am a solid convert.) We call it our Sunday Session, and it simply means taking an hour, each of us alone, to think through and plan the week ahead.

Now, spending an hour each Sunday alone and uninterrupted may sound easy to a single person or to grandparents, but to mothers with young children, the idea may sound outrageous! During a workshop on Sunday Sessions, an irate lady raised her hand and insisted that what we were suggesting was absolutely impossible! "You might just as well say, 'why don't you take the whole day off on Sunday?' as ask us to spend one hour! Why, every minute of my day is spent bathing, dressing, curling, and feeding children, not to mention the time required to prepare the meals and clean up afterward. We have a constant flow of relatives and friends in and out. Sunday is our most hectic day. In fact, every day is like that, except not quite so bad! I just haven't got a minute to myself," she raved on.

She continued to be very vocal throughout the workshop and indicated to us several times what unruly and hard-to-handle children she had. By the end of the class it was obvious to everyone there (but her) that she was a prime example of the need for Sunday Sessions. She desperately needed time to sharpen her saw instead of sawing away until the board burned —with no results other than greater fatigue. When this happens, time controls us and we begin just living days instead making days come alive.

This planning hour is the key to your success for the week. On the weeks when something prevents me from having my Sunday Session, I find that I'm unorganized and irritable. My stress level increases by at least 75 percent. I am solidly converted to the principle that where there is a will, there's a way. Nothing you do during the week is more important than that hour of concentrated planning.

Sometimes it requires getting up earlier than the rest of the family. In our house, Richard does the dishes after the Sunday meal, which certainly gives the rest of us a rest and gives me time to find a door that will lock so that I can have my Sunday Session. At every other time of the week, the kids like to follow me around asking questions or pleading their causes in sibling rivalry cases or asking for Popsicles or showing me their latest "hurts," but during that one hour they have learned over the years that when they knock at the door with a "crisis" all I will say is, "I'm having my Sunday Session; go find Daddy." They get the message! You may have to work to convert Daddy to the principle, but when he sees the positive results and realizes he will have his share of private time, he will likely come around.

One hour may seem like a long time. "Whatever do you do with a whole hour?" I've heard many people ask. "Surely you can plan everything you could possibly think of in twenty minutes!" We have found an hour to be just about the right amount of time. However, I must admit to longing for two or three at times.

The following is an explanation of the procedure that I follow. I emphasize in preface to this that every mother should have her own system. Many mothers have systems that are better for them than mine would be in their situations. The following example is strictly to give you some ideas to draw from as you formulate your own plan.

I'll start at the very beginning. On the first Sunday of every year (and sometimes periodically during the year) we organize our goals for the next period of our lives. We look ahead five years or so and try to imagine what we would like to have accomplished by then. We smile as we try to imagine what the children will each be like in that amount of time, as five years make such a huge difference in the life of a child at any age.

Based on a few five-year goals, we write down some more specific one-year goals. (Since we move quite often and we're almost always in a new situation for the summers, we always set specific summer goals when that time rolls around.)

I keep a special book for Sunday Sessions so that my yearly goals are always visible when I plan shorter-range goals. The first Sunday of each month I take a little extra time to plan the monthly goals before I start on that week. Plans become more and more specific as we get to the weekly and daily goals.

I like to use different shapes as symbols of my goals in different areas. (This is just the system I'm using right now. I've gone through a myriad of different ideas but this one seems to work well for me.)

I've decided that I'm not much good to anybody unless my relationships with myself and with my Heavenly Father are good. Therefore I plan those goals first—in a rectangle at the top of the page.

The circle represents my family goals. I always try to think of something special to do for my husband first, as he is truly my first priority. Sometimes the needs are apparent; sometimes I have to think of something exciting. Then I consider my goals with the children according to their needs. Once a month Rick and I spend an evening together on what we call a "five-facet review." We discuss the success of each individual child, mentally, physically, emotionally, socially, and spiritually. We record areas in which they need help. Usually things are fine in most areas. There are just a few ways we could improve on their situations, so these needs are "programmed" into the monthly and weekly goals.

The triangle represents my goals in fulfilling my responsibility to the Church and those who need help. The diamond represents the goals of "the world"—my world: daily tasks that must be accomplished to keep the home and family running smoothly.

The shapes appear in the order in which I listed them. The first three are relationship goals—with myself, my Heavenly Father, my family, and my fellowmen. The fourth is task oriented. Even organizing them in that order helps, because it is too easy otherwise to get priorities mixed up and let the daily demands overtake the things that are really important.

Of course, every week is very important to progress. But you have to keep in mind that even with careful planning some weeks are great successes and some are "bombs." Your chances of success increase drastically, however, when your objectives are organized in your mind.

Following is a picture of a typical Sunday Session on paper. The *goals* appear in the shapes at the top. The *plans* appear on

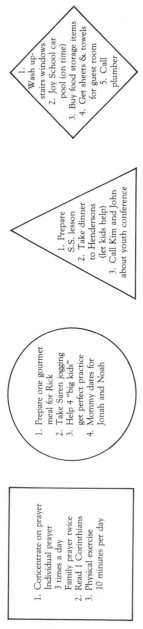

**Shapes (goals):**

Rectangle:
1. Concentrate on prayer
   Individual prayer
   3 times a day
   Family prayer twice
2. Read 1 Corinthians
3. Physical exercise
   10 minutes per day

Circle:
1. Prepare one gourmet meal for Rick
2. Take Saren jogging
3. Help 4 "big kids" get perfect practice
4. Mommy dates for Jonah and Noah

Triangle:
1. Prepare S.S. lesson
2. Take dinner to Hendersons (let kids help)
3. Call Kim and John about youth conference

Diamond:
1. Wash upstairs windows
2. Joy School car pool (on time)
3. Buy food storage items
4. Get sheets & towels for guest room
5. Call plumber

| SUNDAY | MONDAY | TUESDAY | WEDNESDAY | THURSDAY | FRIDAY | SATURDAY |
| --- | --- | --- | --- | --- | --- | --- |
| Prayer (Individual and family) | 6:00 Up—Get ready! | Prayer | Prayer | Prayer | Prayer | Sleep in! |
| 9:00-12:00 Church meetings | Prayer | Morning schedule | Morning schedule | Morning schedule | Morning schedule | Prayer |
| Teach Sunday School | 6:30-7:30 Practice w/kids | | | 7:45 Jog with Saren | | Make list and divide Saturday's work |
| | 7:30 Breakfast | | | | | |
| | 8:00 Get Saren out door Give Josh music lesson while other kids do dishes | | | | | |
| | 8:30 Take kids to school—Jog 10 minutes | | | | | |

**Sunday**
Prayer (Individual)
Sunday dinner
Sunday Sessions for everyone
Write to Grandma
Get kids to do letters and write in journals
Family scripture and discussion
Prayer (Individual and family)
Dinner
7:30 Fireside
Call Kim and John

**Monday**
9:00 Call plumber
9:15 Joy School car pool / Run errands
11:45 Pick up kids
12:00 Read scriptures while kids eat lunch / Prepare soup and bread
3:30 Kids get home / Talk about school
4:00 Cub Scouts
5:30 Special dinner
6:30 Family home evening / Family prayer
7:30 Bedtime / Reading time

**Tuesday**
9:00 Jog 10 minutes
9:30 Get food storage items
12:00 Read scriptures / Prayer
1:00 Prepare dinner with Talmadge / Gourmet dinner for Rick
3:30 Kids home
4:00 Electronics class for Josh / Take Jonah for Mommy date
5:30 Dinner / Prayer
TCJ meeting

**Wednesday**
9:00 Jog 10 minutes
9:15 Joy School car pool / Get towels and sheets
11:45 Pick up kids
12:00 Read scriptures / Prayer / Prepare dinner
2:30 Dentist for Shawni
3:30 Kids home / Homework
4:30 Mommy date for Noah
5:30 Dinner / Family prayer
7:00 Orchestra rehearsal for Saren / Prayer

**Thursday**
9:00 Prepare dinner for us and Hendersons (Noah and Talmadge help)
10:30 Wash upstairs windows
12:00 Read scriptures / Prayer
1:00 Prepare Sunday School lesson while Noah sleeps / Talmadge and Jonah play
3:30 Kids home / Take food to Hendersons
4:00 Shawni's art class
6:00 Dinner / Family prayer
8:00 Meeting with Oswalds

**Friday**
9:00 Jog 10 minutes
9:15 Do washing. Keep at it till it's done!
12:00 Pick up kids and run to Jr. High to do sectional rehearsal for orchestra
2:00 Get Jonah off to birthday party
3:30 Mommy date for Noah—to grocery store
4:30 Take kids ice skating / Dinner / Family prayer
9:30 Movie

**Saturday**
1:00 Rick takes kids to Daddy date—store / Prepare Sunday dinner
Baths
Dinner / Family prayer
7:00 Watch TV special with kids

the daily chart. In other words, first you decide what you want to do, then you decide on the exact day and time to do it! Don't be discouraged when a plan for ten minutes of physical exercise at 6:15 A.M. every day is foiled because the baby was up all night. Just make up your mind to get it done before you go to bed, or, in dire situations, to do twenty minutes tomorrow.

When you get your goals and plans written down, half the battle is won! It's sort of like writing down a grocery list: If you write it down and then forget to take the list, you can still remember most things when you get to the store.

Just having those goals organized in your mind is invaluable. Of course, more things come up in a week than you can possibly write down or calculate. Sometimes not everything on the list gets accomplished, but if you have a framework and if you are sure that your priorities are in proper perspective, the advantages are immeasurable. That frantic feeling of having more to do than you can handle and of losing control of your time is cut to a minimum.

CHALLENGE

There are 168 hours in every week. Take one of those hours every Sunday to plan your week. Arrange a tradeoff with your husband so you can each have your individual hour. If your husband is not at home, have older children tend the younger ones, or even hire a baby sitter if necessary, so that you can sharpen your saw. Plan everything from your priorities to your menus. Plan to fulfill your needs and the needs of your family and friends. Remember that it's much better to plan and partially fail than not to plan at all. Use a planning method that best fits your own family and its lifestyle—but *plan!*

---

## 3. Get Lost and Find Yourself

I'm a great believer in solitude and its absolute necessity to the effective mother. This section goes beyond the one hour of concentration time on Sunday to a few additional hours a week or sometimes an extended period of solitude.

William James described a woman's life as more and more a state of *Zerrissenheit*, a German word meaning torn-to-pieces-hood. We have to take time to turn our thoughts inward—to think and to contemplate our direction and our intent—before we can be of any help to others.

One of the summers we were able to live at Bear Lake, Rick had a six-week assignment in Salt Lake, so he had to spend three and one-half days with us and three and one-half days in Salt Lake every week. My mother lived nearby (I was born and raised in the area), and going into Montpelier to have fun with her, weed her garden, and get groceries provided a nice break a couple of times a week.

We had just come from Washington, D.C., for the summer and the time was passing quickly. Even though it was a change, the schedule remained demanding. There were still seven little mouths to feed three times a day, a baby that still woke up three times a night, and a cabin to try to keep in some semblance of order with anywhere from nine to thirty-five bodies tracking sand and dirt and towels in and out all day.

Our oldest two girls practiced on violin and piano every day and I tried to do some music theory with the oldest four children every morning. The "big kids" also loved cooking something new every afternoon, and Saren, our oldest, needed to be instructed in her efforts to make her first dress.

Everything was lovely for five weeks, and then suddenly I could feel myself becoming irritable with everybody. My temper started flaring over little things, and the children's arguments and whining really got on my nerves until I felt like clobbering somebody.

Rick noticed my bad moods and asked what was wrong, but I couldn't really tell him. One Sunday evening he sent me to the beach to do some writing. I walked down to the shore and enjoyed the unending and ever-changing beauties of the lake, the sand, the mountains, and the wide expanse of cloudless, brilliant blue sky.

It made an immediate difference in my feelings. I realized that I had never in the entire five weeks walked away to be on my own. I had never enjoyed that beautiful sight without a baby wriggling on my hip or a husband needing a boat driver so he could water-ski or the children yelling, "Hey, Mom, watch me swim!"

At first I felt angry about that discovery, and then, as I analyzed how it could have happened, I realized that it was mostly my fault. We mothers tend to get in a rut. Most days the responsibility and privilege of caring for children is ours, as our husbands go off to support the family. We get accustomed to that and fail to realize that it doesn't have to be that way every day.

It takes a conscientious effort from husband and wife and children to occasionally change the pattern. A mother can be a lot more effective the rest of the week if she has a few hours off to just do her own thing. Though my good husband had been wonderful to see that I got that time away while we were in Washington, our schedule had changed for the summer and we had all kind of forgotten about it.

I knew that I needed time to be alone—out of the house and away—at least once a week, but I had let myself get bogged down with always seeing that my job never ended. Somebody always needed me and couldn't get along without me. Even with only four rooms in our little cabin to take care of (and the children really did most of it) there was still a hard-to-get-rid-of compulsion to wash or clean or teach or preach.

When I got to "my place" on the beach I wrote the following poem, which helped me to sort things out:


*Lonesome*

For weeks it seems
I've been:
    Cleaning cupboards
    Cleaning floors
    Cleaning faces
    Cleaning sores

Sorting clothes
Sorting needs
Sorting garbage
Sorting pleas

Mending armholes
Mending ceilings
Mending knees
Mending feelings

Cooking cakes
Cooking corn
Cooking self
Cooking—worn

Getting stepped on
Getting messed on
Getting oozed on
Getting bruised on

I've been surrounded by:

Arguing children
Creative children
Begging children
Laughing children
Practicing children
Crying children
Caring children
Adorable children
Others' children
Demanding children
And
Talkative friends
Concerned friends
Interesting friends
Dinner friends
Tennis friends

Drop-in friends
Book-writing friends
Knife-making friends
Farm friends
And
Loving husband
Demanding husband
Creative husband
Understanding husband
Un-understanding husband
Exciting husband
All-consuming husband

And through it all
I feel something—uneasy
Not really depression
or confusion, or insecurity
(but some)
I think just mostly
loneliness
How strange
—with all that—
lonely?

*Yes!*
Lonely for myself:
Time to think
and create
and analyze:
cleaning
sorting
cooking
getting
children
friends
husband
alone

A real feeling
　Just like being homesick—
　　Because once I'm "back"
　　I'm new again.
　　　Secure again
　　　Ready to go again.

We mothers have to be "selfish" (or selfless, depending on which way you look at it) enough at least once a week to spend some time alone. And again, I'm convinced that where there's a will there's a way.

On the mornings that Rick was there I could have jumped up just before he reached for his fishing pole and said that I was going jogging or down to the beach to write for a while. Even better, I could have arranged it with him the night before so the fish wouldn't have to be disappointed that he didn't come. Although it seemed impossible at the time, I could have put the older children in charge during the baby's nap and left—even if it was for only half an hour (that baby's a short napper). I could have worked out all sorts of things. I guess I just either had a "martyr's complex" or else I didn't even realize my dilemma. Even my sacred hour on Sunday had not been used very well because of our schedule change. And I had waited until I became a grouchy old bear and miserable to be around before I finally realized it.

In *Gift From the Sea*, Anne Morrow Lindbergh advocates this kind of escape. She says:

"Every person, especially every woman, should be alone sometime during the year, some part of each week, and each day. How revolutionary that sounds and how impossible of attainment. . . . By and large, mothers and housewives are the only workers who do not have regular time off. They are the great vacationless class. . . . If women were convinced that a day off or an hour of solitude was a reasonable ambition, they would find a way of attaining it." (New York: Vintage Books, 1965, pages 48-49.)

Every mother probably has different needs. During the normal school year, when I usually have three preschoolers to "play with" all day, I find that I have to get in the car once a day (or at least walk around outside for a while) to free my mind for a few minutes. There are many ways to accomplish that end, but the important realization is that it must be done.

If your husband doesn't offer, point out your need (I know that's sometimes the hardest part) and work out a deal with him whereby he can take the kids (yes, even the baby) sometimes on Saturday or Sunday for a few hours so that you can be alone. If your husband just isn't available, get a baby sitter. Spend your time well and you'll be a new wife and mother by the time you return. Somehow it's much easier to bear down and work hard if you know there will be a break at the end of the line—before you have to begin again.

We asked a bright couple with eleven children how they survived. They smiled knowingly and the father said, "You know, it really is hard at times to keep yourself together with the rigorous demands of career and children. It's equally or probably even more demanding for my wife. Mary's career is the children and the household—a never-ending, always demanding career. We found that our most valuable possession was our little playhouse, just out of sight in the back yard, with one single bed. When one of us got to the point where he or she couldn't take any more, that one would say, 'I've had it! I'm going to the playhouse!' The other would understand as the frustrated parent grabbed blanket and pillow and headed for the secret hiding place. The children knew they were not to disturb that person until he or she returned."

We have used that philosophy several times in our marriage. When we were in England on our mission, we had jurisdiction over the channel islands between England and France. About once every three months I flew down twenty-four hours before our scheduled meetings, either all by myself or with a nursing baby, and simply dove into the writing and reading I'd been dying to do—only coming up occasionally for food and a jog along the beach. The next two days Richard joined me for meetings, and then he stayed an extra twenty-four hours to write and read after I had returned to the mission home.

I think I accomplished more in establishing goals and thinking about relationships with my husband and children during those concentrated times than I had at any other time.

Another example: One year Richard went on a ten-day trip to Washington, D.C. When he got home I was fit to be tied and wondered if I was still in my right mind!

Richard could see that I was about to collapse, so he immediately called a nearby hotel, made a reservation, and sent me away with the nursing baby for twenty-four hours to spend as I saw fit. It was so wonderful that I could hardly believe it. Just before I left, I confided in two friends who happened to be with me at an aerobics class that I was going away for a whole day to be myself. Obviously, neither caught the gist of the program. One said, "Are you having trouble sleeping?" She was evidently very puzzled and secretly wondering if this was a trial separation. The other shuddered and said, "Oh, I don't know what I'd ever do with myself."

With a great sense of freedom and joy, I checked into the hotel at about noon and immediately got some sleep—something I hadn't had enough of for two and one-half months, ever since the baby was born. Renewed, I pushed the baby to a nearby shopping mall and spent two hours just shopping for myself, spending the Christmas money I hadn't had time to use. What a wonderful feeling!

I was anxious, however, to get to my writing, so I stuffed down a hot dog and a couple of chocolate-chip cookies and went back to the hotel and read and wrote and watched the news and slept! How lovely!

The baby was wonderful during the night, requiring only to have the pacifier pushed back into his mouth a few times, and slept until 6:00 A.M. I fed him, slept again, got up and washed my hair—for the first time in two weeks. What an exhilarating feeling it was to get just me and one other person ready!

With a little time left to get a prescription and the groceries and presents I needed for two birthday parties, I was ready to face the next day. I went home a new woman. I had stepped back and looked at my life and at how very blessed I was! I had set goals for myself and my relationships with husband and children. I had had time to read scriptures for a while and to pray meaningfully, not just for a few minutes at the beginning and end of each day. It was heavenly!

Let me emphasize here that I realize my husband is very different from many husbands. Not every husband could or would stay with children for a whole day (especially during the week), and so other arrangements must be made. A mother, a sister, or even a neighbor might be willing to help if you asked or offered a trade of some sort. Your husband may even surprise you if you lay it all out on the table and tell him exactly how you feel. Sometimes it is hard for husbands (as it is for us) to see our needs until we present them in a rational, organized way.

Again in *Gift From the Sea,* (page 42) Mrs. Lindbergh writes with great perception and clarity about solitude:

"It is a difficult lesson to learn today—to leave one's friends and family and deliberately practice the art of solitude for an hour or a day or a week. For me, the break is the most difficult. Parting is inevitably painful, even for a short time. . . . And yet, once it is done, I find there is a quality to being alone that is incredibly precious. Life rushes back into the void, richer, more vivid, fuller than before."

CHALLENGES

1. Find time to be alone. Get help from your husband, mother, sister, or baby sitter. Don't say you don't have time. Make time! It is more important than almost anything that you can do to be a better wife and mother. Find a short time each week and an extended period every few months.

2. When you find the time, use it wisely. Enjoy the time it takes to just unwind. Then use the remainder to create your goals and plans—in essence, write your diary in advance.

3. Use the renewing influence of this solitude to improve your relationship with yourself as well as with your husband,

children, family, and friends. Certain springs can only be tapped when you are alone.

## 4. Teach Your Children Responsibility

There are many specific ways to cut down on stress in a normal hectic household. Probably one of the most vital is to share the workload with husband and children. Although this will almost inevitably produce mass pandemonium initially, it's worth sticking to it until the process becomes expected and routine. Don't despair, no matter what, because as children learn to accept responsibility—from the tiny beginnings of the two-year-old being able to get a diaper for the baby to the big things like doing a good job cleaning the bathroom—it is so much the better for everybody involved.

Many times we say to ourselves in exasperation, "I could do it so much faster and easier myself!" Just remember—it's worth the time and trouble in the long run to teach children responsibility. Don't tire yourself by trying to get children to do things beyond their ability. There seems to be a certain breakthrough point (different with each child) at which a child can truly be responsible for his own things and for specific household duties.

It lightens your load and cuts stress in half, when you see unexpected visitors pull in the driveway, if you can shout: "Saren, do the hall; Shawni, clear the downstairs; Josh, do the guest bathroom; Saydi, clear the kitchen—quick!" and be pretty confident that if you meet your friends on the front doorstep and chat about their "exciting" surprise visit for about two minutes, things will be at least respectable if not pleasantly orderly by the time they step in the front door.

Of course, I say that with my tongue in cheek—but it is truly wonderful to see everybody pitch in with the work.

Since Richard and I have written a book (*Teaching Children Responsibility*, Salt Lake City: Deseret Book Co., 1982) that goes into great detail about responsibility, I will not attempt to do that here. However, I have so often been asked about our children's responsibilities that I will give a brief sketch, knowing that each household is very different (many do a better job than ours) and that each year our responsibilities change.

Our two older girls get up in time to be dressed and ready for violin practicing by 6:15 A.M. They have their own alarm clock so that I can get myself ready quickly while they begin. We have ensemble practice (with me on the viola and Daddy on the cello) at 6:30. Then, while I give at least one music lesson to one of them, our next two children get themselves dressed and cook breakfast (their music lessons are in the afternoon). I also work on hair and diapers, dress the preschoolers, and help with the last-minute breakfast details so that we can kneel for prayer at 7:30 and be finished with breakfast and have the four older children ready to walk out the door to catch the bus at 8:00.

It may sound like a hurried schedule, but if we start on time we even have time for an emergency or two without too much hassle.

There is usually an absolute disaster here and there, and though the older children usually leave their rooms in perfect order and take pride in them, the younger ones only occasionally manage to get to their rooms. We're still working on that!

After school one child is assigned a quick "run through" on the upstairs, another on the downstairs, meaning that they straighten rooms and pick up the things that are out of place. Another child is expected to get all the garbage gathered and put out, and another to clean one bathroom. Each child is also expected to have a clean room. At dinner time the plates are turned upside-down, and the children are not allowed to turn them over until their jobs are completed.

After dinner one child cleans the table, another does dishes, another sweeps the floor, and another empties the dishwasher.

Before they go to bed, each child sets out his clothes for the next day, brushes his teeth, and says prayers.

All these responsibilities are simplified by what we call our "peg board." It is a three-dimensional board with four holes below each child's name, into which pegs are plugged when each job is completed. The first peg represents morning responsibilities; the next, practicing; the third, daily job; and the fourth, nighttime responsibilities.

This pegboard (also explained in more detail in *Teaching Children Responsibility*) has simplified the concept of responsibility in the children's minds, and when those pegs are in they feel a certain sense of real satisfaction (and my everyday stress and strain diminishes greatly).

Let me hasten to add once again that every peg does not get put in every day, and it takes a great deal of remembering and reminding yourself to remind the children at first, but it gets easier!

One of the great keys to making this work is having the support and help of your husband. Although the mother is there more of the time and therefore is usually the taskmaster, a firm reminder from Daddy and frequent urgings from him about the importance of fulfilling responsibilities can do wonders.

Another valuable tool is the actual help of the father. Our daddy helps where he can during the week, but he always gives us all a rest and does the dishes on Sunday. This began on the first week of our marriage as a kind gesture and has turned into a tradition that the children would never let him forget.

Although I have emphasized the struggle many times, we have discovered over the years that children will do exactly what they know is expected of them. If they understand these expectations when they are young, life gets easier rather than harder as they get older.

You can make the task more fun by changing systems or rewards occasionally to keep minds and hands excited. I will not include elaborate systems here, although there are many. Use one that children and parents both feel excited about.

One of our greatest finds in teaching children responsibility came from a school near our home in Washington. Because there were not enough available mothers or teacher's aides to hear the children in the early grades read, they solicited the aid of the older students who were doing well to come in and listen for a few minutes several times a week. Our children considered it a great honor to be asked to be a "tutor." Both tutor and "tutee" loved the program and learned a great deal.

We decided to let this great natural love children have for younger children come into play in our own family.

When a child reaches the age of eight a big transition takes place at our house. He or she becomes one of "the adults." They attend an adult planning meeting each Sunday night in which we plan our strategy for the "little kids" during the coming week. Every month one of these children is assigned to be a tutor for one of the children under eight. This means that he sits by him at the dinner table and helps him with his food if necessary. He sees that his "tutee's" teeth are brushed and bed is made, and acts as his partner on excursions to the zoo or shopping. He helps him put his pajamas on and tucks him in bed, ready for Mom or Dad to listen to prayers.

The tutors receive extra points in the family point system for their tutees, depending on how good a job they do.

There is nothing more fun than watching a nine-year-old try to help his three-year-old tutee to brush his teeth. I must admit that since we enlisted the "other" adults' help, our job has become markedly easier. Every month we exchange tutors and tutees so everybody gets a chance to help or learn from everybody else. It is wonderful to watch the growth on the part of both tutor and tutee! For those of you who don't have anybody who is eight yet, hang on—help is coming!

CHALLENGES

1. Set a daily schedule and live it. Make adjustments when necessary, but don't let the exceptions become the rule.

2. Read *Teaching Children Responsibility.*

3. Have a "tutor and tutee" system if you have some children over eight and some under. Make older children part of the solution rather than part of the problem.

---

## 5. Expect Respect

We live in a permissive society! Sometimes the permissiveness creeps into our own homes without our even realizing it.

I recall an experience I had when we had just arrived in England. Joyce, an outspoken young English girl who was helping me one day, couldn't help hearing a rather heated conversation between me and our oldest daughter, Saren (who was six). After it was over and Saren had disappeared, Joyce said to me, "Why do you let Saren talk to you like that?"

"Like what?" I asked, amazed that she would think it was peculiar.

"Like she did this afternoon when you were 'having words' with her. Americans seem to let their children speak to them in such a dreadful manner!"

I was shocked, but I've come to be grateful to Joyce for that question, because it might otherwise have taken me quite some time to recognize that Saren really did have a nasty tone in her voice when she disagreed with me. She had been speaking with near contempt. I simply had tuned out the offensiveness in her voice because I'd heard it often. But, in thinking about it, I decided that Joyce was absolutely right and that things were going to change.

"It's all right to ask questions," I told Saren that evening, "but you must remember to use a respectful tone of voice." Occasionally she ventures too near the line, but when I give her a certain signal, she remembers and calms down.

The bottom line in getting respect from your children (other than the obvious one of deserving it) is that they will give you exactly as much as you expect.

Two other vital ingredients are: (1) Begin when the children are very young. When children are ten it is too late. They must understand clearly from the beginning that there is a certain tone of voice that is not acceptable in your family. (2) Enlist the support of the father. If he is always aware of the slightest tone of disrespect to his wife from the children, one stern statement: "Don't ever speak to your Mommy like that!" does wonders.

If children know that a certain level of respect must always be maintained in the home, the stress level inevitably drops. This is something that is easily overlooked but adds much to having a consistently better spirit in your home.

CHALLENGE

Step back and listen to the tone of voice used commonly in your home. If it is undesirable, design a plan to do something about it. Remember that kindness and consideration begin with you. How do *you* sound when you're angry or irritated? (Listen to your children sometimes when they're arguing and—possibly to your chagrin—you'll find out.)

# Chapter Four

# More Stress Reducers

$I$s your tension level still too high? Hang on—here are five more ideas that will help.

## 6. Simplify (Not Super Mom, Just Happy Mom)

Simplify—what a great key this word is in coping with stress! There is a way to simplify everything. Try turning things around and thinking in terms of how little, not how much, you can get along with.

The lives of most people in America today are cluttered with too many "things." Even those who can't afford them are duped by the advertising schemes in the media and fill their lives with unnecessary things.

Having fallen into the same pit, we are often glad when we are required to move from one home to the other, because it allows us to get rid of all our excess things. We can never believe all the junk we have collected over the years.

There are broken toys that we kept thinking we would mend, puzzles with missing pieces that I *knew* we could find, books with torn pages that I rationalized someday the children might look through and enjoy the "other" pictures. There are clothes that no one ever wears and "early-marriage" furniture that we finally, fondly, decide to part with.

In addition to that, we take less than half of our furniture with us to Washington and find that we get along beautifully. Our home is much smaller there and the housework time is cut in half.

When we move back out West for the summer, each of the children brings to our four-room cabin two playsuits, a swimsuit, and one Sunday outfit, and life gets even more pleasant.

Granted, summer and beach life require less clothing, but I am amazed to find that our trips to other places are also simplified, and that amount of clothing was sufficient as long as I had access to a washing machine. (As I remember, the baby had a few extra pieces of clothing—especially pajamas.)

When time for school rolls around, each of the children gets one good pair of shoes and one brand-new outfit to wear the first day. The older children sometimes get more because they pay for their own clothes, and there are a few exceptions when all the boys' knees wear out. This system makes school shopping much more simple (and less expensive).

At Christmas each child gets one gift from Santa Claus and one Christmas outfit. Anything else is "cream."

There are so many ways to simplify.

Simplify Sunday mornings by preparing clothes and food on Saturday. Serve granola bars and prepared orange juice for super-easy preparation and clean-up if your church meetings are early. (We also sometimes serve granola bars, milk, and apples if meetings are late.)

Simplify meals and clean-up on busy days with paper plates, and yes, sometimes even convenience foods.

Simplify Sunday School lessons by using a household item in an object lesson rather than spending hours on elaborate posters and handouts that are forgotten by the morrow anyway.

Simplify errands by finding ways to cut out those that aren't absolutely necessary, and by combining them with other runs.

Simplify toys by getting rid of or at least putting away the ones your children don't love. Don't buy toys with thousands of pieces until their owners can take care of them. Give the children more Scotch tape and paper to create with.

There are a thousand ways to simplify your life if you can think about it long enough to decide how.

Don't give up your favorite things to the point that you feel deprived. For example, I know that an artificial Christmas tree would save time and money at the holiday season, but I can't bear to give up the family fun of going to get the tree, or the smell that means Christmas to me.

If arranging an elaborate table for dinner guests is your "thing," enjoy it—and simplify in other ways (a pizza house that delivers?).

Early in our marriage I really enjoyed preparing elaborate dinners for friends (although I smile when I remember how I used to clean the refrigerator and oven and scrub and wax the kitchen floor every time). Now things get too complicated and out of control, so we rarely have intimate dinners with our friends in our home—only "mob scenes" with tons of kids to throw hamburgers or spaghetti at. I figure that those quiet times will come again, someday.

We have also had many, many study groups in our home. After the discussion a lovely dessert is usually expected, and as most of the time the group rotated homes, each wife would always try to plan something more elegant and delicious than the last. When our lives got too complicated I decided to make a pact with the other wives to serve plain water—or nothing at all. Somehow I enjoyed those discussions much more than usual because I was not worrying about getting out the refreshments before someone had to leave. I actually listened and participated.

Don't let yourself fall into the trap of believing that because all the other mothers throw elaborate birthday parties for their kids, you have to do the same. Do something that's easy but has pizzazz. I remember crying over the dirty stairs one day two hours before a birthday party for our three-year-old because they were littered with everything from popcorn to nails. I was sure everyone at the party (*all* those three-year-olds) would think me a terrible housekeeper if I didn't get my stairs vacuumed. However, I was due to have our third baby any day and was having regular contractions.

What a silly lady! Instead of having the party outside, I complicated things as much as possible and got on the phone and called until I found a teenager in the neighborhood whom I could hire to come and vacuum my stairs. (I guess it could have been worse. *I* could have vacuumed the stairs, gone into hard labor, and had the baby during the party.)

If only I had had the word *simplify* in my mind I could have saved myself a lot of grief as a young mother.

Remember the principle of pizzazz as you simplify. There is a fine line between simplifying and becoming mediocre. Use your creativity and do things with flair but in the simplest form.

CHALLENGES

1. Dare to be different and simplify! It's one of the most timesaving, stress-reducing devices you can find.

2. Start with the things around you. Get rid of the clutter. Put your priorities into perspective. Simplify your own wardrobe as well as the children's. Learn to simplify things in your mind when it seems that there is more to do than you can handle.

3. Cut out unnecessary distractions and don't worry about trying to keep up with the other mothers. In fact, if you simplify effectively, they might want to try it themselves.

---

## 7. Put Your House in Order

"Organize yourselves; prepare every needful thing; and establish a house, even a house of prayer, a house of fasting, a house of faith, a house of learning, a house of glory, a house of order, a house of God" (D&C 88:119).

Since the first year of our married life this scripture has hung in our home, and we have tried (sometimes pitifully) to follow its admonitions. Order is mentioned twice in this verse—at the first and last—and it seems to sort of sandwich everything else.

I have a confession to make. I am not a naturally tidy person. I somehow managed to blunder through high school and college excusing my disastrous room with obligations to practice and leadership responsibilities at school. My dad used to jokingly call me "Mrs. Smith," the name of a particularly disorganized neighbor. (One day I asked to use her phone, and after picking my way through the debris to the phone, I turned around to see their dead Christmas tree still decorated in the corner. It was now March.)

At college I was "blessed" with a roommate who was exactly like me, and though we both did well in school and were gone most of the time studying or practicing, we always returned to a room that looked very much as though someone had thrown a hand grenade in and shut the door. Occasionally I'd turn over a new leaf, but it was short-lived.

It seems to me that I improved for a while after our marriage, thinking how embarrassed I'd be if *he* found out how bad I was. As children came along, however, things began to get muddled again, and I began getting up in the morning to a sink full of dirty dishes that I had been just too tired to wash the night before.

After four children and many, many commitments to try harder, I finally reached the point where I could no longer tolerate the messy rooms at night, the lost shoes, clothes, scissors, papers, and so forth. We decided in earnest that the time had arrived. All the "wouldn't-it-be-nice" ideas were to be implemented. I quickly realized that any plan had to start with me, the mother!

A good friend taught me the principle of touching things only once, which helped me immensely. For example, if your recipe calls for salt, take it from the cupboard, put it in the mix, and return it to the cupboard all in one movement. When washing clothes, put the item straight from the dryer into a basket labeled for the appropriate person. The list goes on and on, but as I implemented the principle, I found that the clutter began to disappear.

All in all, I can honestly say that since I have started putting away all my own things, seeing that my own bed was the first one made, and have followed through with making the children responsible for their things, our home has been a different place. I would not have believed that it could make so much difference!

I am a firm believer in the saying, "Thing order precedes thought order." It is almost impossible for me to get my mind functioning smoothly if I am surrounded with clutter and unable to find anything I need.

In getting your home in order you first must decide what you *really* want. You can do anything you deem absolutely necessary —but it isn't easy. Keep in mind also that one mother's definition of order is very different than another's. "I spend *my* time on the *children*," said one messy mother with a smile. Remember as you think through the process of order in your home that you do have to set standards in your family's mind and then—the hardest part—be consistent. However, you also have to remember, as you grind those rusty wheels of better household order into action and establish a better system, that although you can do anything you really want, you can't do everything.

You can spend so much time on your home, cleaning and putting things in order, that you neglect the children. Find a system that has a happy medium, that produces a comfortable order level but also involves the principle of "selective neglect." I personally don't believe it's possible for a mother with a young family to keep everything perfect all the time. Sometimes, as the "new" saying goes, "It isn't pretty being easy."

Wonderful mothers have produced charts and awards, plans and schemes by the thousands to keep children excited about carrying out responsibilities and keeping things in order. I start thinking that we're doing all right, and then I hear of a new, exciting system that absolutely astounds and inspires me. This book is not designed to give all those elaborate plans, however. My goal here is to encourage you to come up with your own plan, one that you feel comfortable using with your own family. Make your plan exciting for the children and base it on a system with lots of rewards and a few punishments. Then be consistent to help them achieve excellence.

A good friend advocates (and I agree with her) the principle of changing the system of rewards at least every three months to keep the kids excited. The end results remain the same, but the children get a fresh breath of air to try again.

We like to keep our systems fairly simple. Sometimes if things get too elaborate they become a pain instead of a help.

I would like to mention a few basics that have helped us a great deal in establishing better order in our home. After taking a good look at the frequent "disaster areas" (the little ones' rooms) we decided that the biggest culprits were: (1) dressers to hang clothes out of, (2) closets where everything accidentally dropped to the floor, and (3) beds under which to hide toys,

Sunday suits with mashed potatoes squashed on them, school-work, empty dog-food cans, half-eaten appies, and an amazing assortment of other treasures. Our solution may sound a bit extreme, and I'm sure most of you will not be ready to run right out and try this tomorrow, but it might give you some ideas.

Since we were remodeling the kitchen and laundry room of our home anyway, we decided to do it with order and con-venience for *our* family in mind. We enlarged the kitchen in two directions to create a better flow of traffic and to accommodate the hundreds of bodies in and out each week.

Then we decided to turn an unfinished area in the basement into a "nerve center." We removed the dressers from all the chil-dren's rooms except those of the two oldest girls (who do a good job of taking care of their own things) and built a "unit" (see accompanying illustration) in the laundry room for each of the five younger children. Each unit consists of four drawers: one for shirts, one for pants, one for pajamas, and one for underclothes and socks. Under the four drawers we put a bin for shoes. Above the drawers are two square shelves for treasures, school projects, and special possessions, and to the right a tall opening for violins, tennis racquets, and baseball bats. Above that are two shelves that only I (or Dad) can reach: one for seasonal clothes (winter clothes in summer, summer clothes in winter) and the other for hand-me-downs that the child is about to grow into. The units are part of the laundry room so that the children go there, take off dirty clothes, and put them in the appropriate bins (one for darks, one for mediums, and one for whites), and choose clean clothes or pajamas.

When I do the washing, the clothes go directly from the bins to the washer, dryer, folding table, and back into the drawers— all within six or eight steps. There are also two bars for hanging clothes and four shelves for Mom, Dad, and the two big girls where we pick up our things once a week and put them in our rooms.

We also took all the toys out of the rooms and put them in one toy area with shelves and drawers where they belong when not in use.

# THE "UNIT"

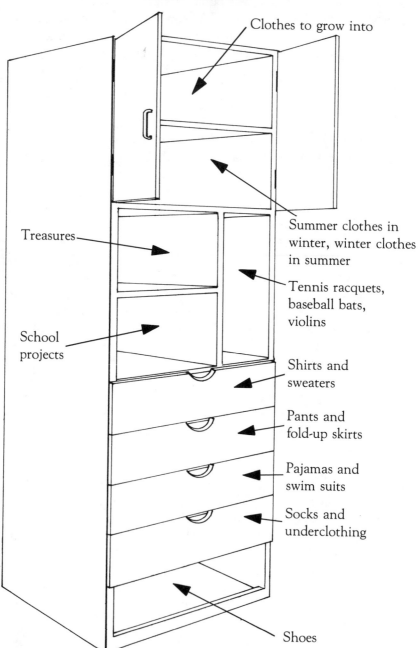

Clothes to grow into

Summer clothes in winter, winter clothes in summer

Tennis racquets, baseball bats, violins

Treasures

School projects

Shirts and sweaters

Pants and fold-up skirts

Pajamas and swim suits

Socks and underclothing

Shoes

With no clothes or toys or dressers in the children's rooms, things became much simpler. Each child has a bed, a nightstand with special books to read at bedtime, and pictures and decorations on the walls that make him happy. We further simplified the rooms of the "super messers" (two little boys) by replacing the traditional beds with chairs that fold out into beds. They use washable sleeping bags on the fold-out beds at night and have a "sitting room" during the day. (Sleeping bags are kept in the closet.)

I admit that the children still manage to cut up bits of paper in their rooms and do a good job once in a while of making a pretty fair mess, but by and large about 75 percent of the clutter is eliminated. They usually take great pride in seeing that their rooms are clean before they go to school because it isn't an insurmountable job. Even our tiny boys (ages three and two) love making their beds (which consists of throwing their continental quilts up around their pillows).

You may not be ready to remodel your home, but consider rearranging it. Put all the dressers in the laundry room and all the toys in a toy room. Don't leave the little children anything to make a mess with. Teach the little ones that their clothes can be in only one of three places: on their bodies, in their units, or in the "dirty bins." As children are old enough to take pride in their things, reward them by moving dressers and toys back into their rooms.

Another major necessity for order in the home (as much as I hate to admit it) is our getting up in the morning. This has been hard for me ever since I was a child and used to get up at 6:00 A.M. and put on my mother's old beaver coat to keep me warm in the cold room where the piano was.

Some mothers of preschoolers love schedules—love getting up early and getting things done before the kids wake up. I'm sorry to report that I'm not one of them. When our little ones were preschoolers, I enjoyed to the fullest my freedom of not having to meet everyday schedules, because I had the feeling that it wouldn't last long—and it didn't!

I basically hate schedules. I hate doing things at the same time every day, but I've learned through the school of hard knocks that for a family with lots of children it's the best way.

To this day I can't wait until the Christmas holidays and summer vacations so that we can just relax and do what we want to do.

I truly envy you who "pop out" at 5:00 A.M. and get it all together. As it is, I do my best to drag myself out at 6:00 (I also love to stay up late) or 6:15 at the latest to make sure the first two practicers are ready to begin on the downbeat of 6:30.

If we have breakfast and a short devotional at 7:30 and get our "junior higher" out the door and rooms checked by 8:00, and everybody off to school on time, I feel as if we've really accomplished something. Maybe that sounds easy to some of you early birds, but for us it's a major project! I've discovered that getting things done in order, the same way every day, helps the children feel secure and orderly.

Another basic rule of thumb is never to go to bed with a dirty kitchen. (By that I mean dirty dishes and clutter.) It took me several years to figure out that it would be much harder to face a sink full of dirty dishes in the morning than it is late at night—no matter *how* tired you are. I remember feeling terribly depressed because it often took me until noon to get the kitchen back in order again after a busy night. (Just in time to mess it up again with lunch.) Even if you are tripping over toys to get there, a clean kitchen is like a breath of encouraging air first thing in the morning.

When you get the kitchen mastered, take a quick run through the rest of the house to be sure things are put away at night. The benefit in the morning is immeasurable. During really busy times we find it also helps to set the breakfast table and prepare the orange juice at night. On school days we have a fairly set menu for each day so that nobody has to wonder what to fix. (Of course there are always those days when you're out of milk *and* eggs, and then a creative idea or two really helps.)

Order is the key to many things in a busy household. Even though I still can rarely find a brush, a pen, or a pair of scissors, I can honestly say that things are getting better.

One other tidbit is the fact that order begins with you. Get yourself ready and your bed made first! Resolve that you're never going to "mush" through the kitchen in your nightgown and bare feet to meet the mailman in your bathrobe again (at least on school days)! It makes everybody feel better about having a good, productive day if you look ready to stand at the helm first thing in the morning.

CHALLENGES

1. Analyze the order situation in your home and decide what needs to be done to improve it. Consult with the kids and then (with a few ideas to guide them) decide together on a system that is fun and rewarding for everyone.

2. Stick to it! It's taken us many years to begin to say that things are *really* getting better (I hope you're all smarter— sooner). After you've reached a satisfactory level of order, remember that everything can't always be perfect. Don't sweat the small stuff.

3. Get up and get going. Get up before the kids, and/or train them so well that things go along smoothly even when you're sick or nursing or pregnant.

---

## 8. Expand Your Horizons

"All work and no play makes Mom a dull girl!" Although it seems just as impossible as anything else extra that there is to do besides cleaning, cooking, and caring for children, it is very important to keep learning, keep growing.

Sometimes a mother feels selfish taking her precious time from the children to do something she wants to do, but I like to think about it the opposite way. It's not only that we are better mothers when we have some creative outlets to free our minds periodically—the most important reason for our growing and progressing is because it helps the children. We can only teach what we know. The greater the variety of interests to which we can expose our children, the better educated they are. Don't leave it all up to someone else!

Of course, I'm not implying that we all should go back to school full time so that we can teach our children art or economics. The time for that (for most of us) has passed for a while. But there is an abundance of things that you can do to enrich your life—even *with* a troop of small children.

Find ways to actively use the gifts you've been given. If you're an artist, start an art class among mothers for fun and enjoyment. If you love to read, create a book club that meets once a month to discuss a certain preassigned book. If you love cooking, create a rotating dinner group and perhaps choose food from another country once a month to share together. If you love dancing, find a neighbor or relative who can take your children for just two hours once a week, and dance away. Or take an aerobics class—often nurseries are provided.

It is always easier not to get involved in the hassle of arranging things and getting the kids ready and out the door, but the extra effort is almost always worth it!

My particular love is music. I was a string major in college, and though I was terrified to play by myself, I loved playing in groups. Many years ago, when we were first married, I found a wonderful group of "kindred spirits" while we lived in Washington, D.C., with whom I played in a string quartet. It was their love and support that changed my terror of performing into a love for it. The group consisted of another violinist, Cheryln; a cellist, Carolyn; and a violist, another Carolyn. (I always regretted that my name wasn't Marilyn.)

Richard and I moved away from these "soul sisters" for almost eight years, and then went back to Washington to find that they were all still there, ready to play. Our circumstances had changed somewhat by then, however: Among the four of us we had twenty-six children and two grandchildren.

After our first rehearsal we were so thrilled to be playing together again that we pledged ourselves to prepare a forty-five-minute program to be presented in three months (before we moved again) at the Washington Temple Visitors' Center.

No one would believe the riotous times we had together at rehearsals. If we could have taped the practices, unedited they would easily have been funnier than any sitcom you see on TV.

In the first place, we rehearsed with at least seven preschoolers under foot. (We learned to practice with our feet on our stands to keep the crawling babies from tipping them over.) One Carolyn was the president of a large women's organization and dashed in between meetings to play. The other Carolyn had to drive forty-five minutes one way to get to the rehearsals and came in her teenager's car (which looked a lot like it had just been through the trash masher) in between car-pools and the frantic schedules of her eight children. Cheryln had a nursing baby, and though we tried to convince her to learn to nurse and play the violin at the same time (mothers have to learn to do almost any *other* two actions simultaneously) she opted to hum her part while we played and she nursed.

Someone was always late, and there were usually two or three rounds of calls before we worked out a satisfactory "next rehearsal" time. But when we got together—did we ever have a great time! We loved making beautiful music together.

Every rehearsal was an adventure. About every eight minutes one of the roving pack of little ones needed a Band-Aid, a rescue from a bad dog, a peanut-butter sandwich, a clean diaper, or a mediator for negotiations on toys. Other than that, they danced together to the music and once even took off all their clothes and had a great romp in the little plastic swimming pool in the back yard. At the end of the movement, Carolyn often found my baby hanging on the endpin of her cello, gazing up at her.

We performed many times together during those few months and it was always an unbelievable hassle, but the night of our *big* recital topped them all in more ways than one.

One Carolyn had just returned from a two-week trip to Hawaii, China, and Egypt, and we had practiced ferociously the last two days. The night of the performance she called to ask if I could drive, as she had just realized that the insurance had expired on her car. I had been about to call her to tell her that there was a flat tire on our car and we had no spare. I had been frantically packing all day in 90-degree heat and 85-percent humidity, as the moving men were coming the next day. We decided on the uninsured car.

When we got there, a little later than planned, the other Carolyn and Cheryln, who came from the other direction, still had not arrived, and when they did (huffing and puffing and red-faced) one explained that her husband had been held up and didn't get home to take over the kids and the other had a van full of cases of grapefruit that her kids were selling for a fund-raising project. Somehow the brake had released and the van had coasted across the street and into the neighbor's tree, scattering grapefruits everywhere, not to mention the damage to car and tree. We all got the giggles about being so "true to the end" and then settled down to the seriousness of the task ahead.

I must admit that my eyes filled with tears during the last piece we played, "Canon in D" by Johann Pachelbel, a work that we all loved. My mind wandered back to all the wonderful times we'd had together talking and playing and enjoying in spite of the adversity. How easy it would have been for any *one* to say, "I'm too busy. Let's do that when the kids are grown." (In this case we knew it was now or never.)

Of course there are many things that we do have to give up at certain times in our child-raising years. Only you can judge when the children are suffering rather than benefiting from a too-busy, too-strung-out mom. Do the things that you really feel will benefit you *and* the children most. If your desires require your kids to spend long hours with a baby sitter for an extended period, you might want to wait.

Another way to expand your horizons is to form a mothers' group, a group of young mothers with whom you feel very comfortable. Start small, two or three will do, or go to five or six if there is a natural group that seems to jell. Then do something more than just go out to lunch together! I'm convinced that women are a great comfort and help to one another—even women with wonderful husbands and no major problems.

The first group that I was involved in was such great fun! We were all young moms with one or two tiny children. We met together once a month and set some common goals. We all decided that our biggest problems were (1) getting up early enough in the morning and (2) reading the scriptures daily. We decided what time we needed to get up to be effective (times ranged from 5:00 A.M. to 7:30) and we also decided on a certain amount of scriptures to read before we met again. We called each other periodically to "check up." We all made great progress.

Another group formed in a different location spent time talking about everything from food storage to child discipline. Still another group concentrated more on reading something each month that was particularly pertinent to the pressures of mothering, and then discussing it.

Each woman in each of these groups has a special, warm place in my heart for the things that she taught me. It was wonderful to discover that other mothers were struggling with the same things I was, and often had solutions I hadn't thought of.

The group I'm involved with now has decided to have each woman read independently on a different subject each month and then report to the others on her findings. Last month we talked about "inspiring women"; we hope to get into things like political figures and the lives of composers and artists. It's impossible to do all the reading that you'd like to when children are small, but it's nice to have some help and at the same time to form eternal friendships.

## Learn, Then Teach

Among all the hats that a mother must wear—cook, cleaner, car-pooler, negotiator, washer, sorter, repair person—there is one hat that may be more important than all the others put together: the teacher's hat.

It is easy to get priorities mixed up and to spend 99 percent of our time struggling with the things that seem most pressing while neglecting the things that are most valuable and enduring.

It has been said that children never stop learning, even for a moment. But *what* they are learning is not always what we think we are teaching. We teach by example every day, and sometimes the children are learning things that we'd rather not have them know, such as how to manipulate people, how to get mad, or how to be continually late.

We should take our jobs as teachers very seriously and not limit our teaching to the things that children happen to learn through example. We should decide what we want our children to learn and then go for it!

Contrary to what we would sometimes like to think, school and church do not teach our children all that they need to know. Parents must supplement and stimulate!

We can't teach everything at once. Selecting "majors" and "minors" each year for your family can help. (This is explained in more detail in chapter 5.)

Most public schools, for all their good points, do not do an adequate job of teaching communication skills (writing, reading, speaking, listening), of teaching the skills of questioning and research, or of teaching the arts.

Of course many volumes could be written about teaching these subjects to children in your home. The greatest questions are *when* and *how*. We have found that we are able, at least three times a week, to be all together around the dinner table and to conduct fifteen-to-twenty-minute educational sessions for the children. On Mondays, we start these dinner sessions with speeches. Each child stands, in turn, and speaks extemporaneously on an assigned topic for sixty seconds. On Wednesdays, we start dinner with "the question game," in which Dad or Mom mentions a topic and each child asks the best question he can think of on that topic. This often leads us to the family encyclopedias for some interesting research after dinner. On Fridays, the children write short themes or poems which they read to the family during dinner.

In addition to dinner time, use the time when children are just home from school. As they unwind from a hectic day, have them dance to or listen to great music instead of letting them become glued to the "know-nothing nonsense" on TV.

Much of the real joy in parenting comes from teaching children to appreciate the finer things in life through music, art, dance, and literature. Often the greatest challenge for this type of teaching is that we must first educate ourselves. Few things can lift the spirit to "the higher realm" more quickly than the fine

arts. Even if it takes extra time and effort for us to educate ourselves, the return is invaluable.

Let me suggest some simple methods in each area that may
spark some ideas of your own.

*Art:* While visiting with some friends a few years ago I
noticed nine small prints of famous paintings on the wall of the
family room. When I inquired about them the mother stated
that the family was studying art together. Every member of the
family (from mom and dad down to the three-year-old) knew
who had painted each picture and what kind of picture it was
(classic, impressionistic, and so on). Their three-year-old pointed
out her favorite, and when asked who painted it she answered
with a smile, "Mikoangewo."

We can appreciate the world much more fully if we educate
ourselves and our children to see the beauty of art—including
color, form, and texture.

*Music:* The amount of wonderful music to which you can
expose your children is almost endless, but try starting with one
of these well-loved classics (easily found in most libraries): "Peter
and the Wolf," by Sergei Prokofiev; "The Planets," by Gustav
Holtz; "Pictures at an Exhibition," by Modest Mussorgsky; "The
Sorcerer's Apprentice," by Paul Dukas; or "Ride of the
Valkyries," "Forest Murmurs," or "The Magic Fire Music" from
*The Ring* by Richard Wagner.

Do some research (there is usually quite a lot of information
on the backs of the album covers) on the pieces and explain the
"stories" to your children as you play them. Learn to love them
together and fine music will be a treasure throughout your lives.

When you can, expose your children to live concerts and
artists. Don't try to do too much at once. (Try leaving at inter-
mission before your "Cub Scouts" become restless—and go for
ice cream.)

*Dance:* There are two simple ways for children to appreciate
dance: to watch it and to do it. We are always amazed at how
exciting it is to watch our children dance. Put on any of the
pieces of music just mentioned, or one of your own favorites, and
watch their personalities pop out before your very eyes. Boys and

girls, young and old alike cannot help but have an exciting experience in making their bodies move to beautiful music.

If you have an opportunity to take them to a ballet, such as
*The Nutcracker* or *Swan Lake*, check out or purchase beforehand
a good recording of the ballet to use as "background music" for
your daily activities for a couple of weeks. You'll be amazed at
the difference it makes if the music is familiar.

*Literature:* In our opinion, one of the greatest series of books
a child can read (on his own from about age ten) or have read to
him (down to age three) is *The Chronicles of Narnia* by C. S.
Lewis. Not only are these tales well written, but the principles of
life taught therein are wonderful.

Of course a list of the Newbery Award winners is an excellent guide to good reading. Every child should read *Charlotte's
Web* and (every girl at least) *The Little Princess*, but don't limit
yourself to those. There are many wonderful classics available
that are extremely enlightening and enriching for young children
to give them a head start on their formal education in leterature.

One summer I read with our eleven-year-old *A Tale of Two
Cities* by Charles Dickens. Although a good dictionary and a lot
of explanations were necessary, it was a wonderful experience for
us both.

One marvelously effective way to get children to read is to
give them a choice between reading and going to sleep. While we
were in England we got used to the practice of early bedtimes.
Our children now know that they must observe a specific (and
rather early) bedtime, but that they have a full hour before lights
out *if* they wish to use it for reading.

In short, remember that the greatest gift you can give your
children is a knowledge of the wonders and beauties found in the
finer things of life. In imparting these things, we expand our own
horizons and can feel ourselves learning and growing as mothers.

CHALLENGES

1. Discover ways to expand your horizons. Use your gifts
before they are taken from you. Decide what would best benefit

you and your children at this point in time and go after it tenaciously.

2. Form a mothers' group with inspiring friends who can help you to expand your horizons.

3. Turn off the TV and *read*.

4. Learn, then teach. Concentrate on one area at a time. Do some research on each subject so that you can teach it more effectively. Bring a "higher realm" to your home by exposing your children to the fine arts.

---

## 9. Guard Your Most Valuable Possession — Your Body

*What's wrong with me?* I thought at the end of a grueling day with the children. *Why can't I get this family going? It seems that all I do all day is give ignored instructions and try to squelch arguments. I'm just the fire extinguisher around here!*

For several weeks it seemed that every child, each half hour or so, went the rounds from getting a finger smashed in a door to getting shoved or banged by a sibling to being "*starving*." When all seven got going at once, I felt like the old woman in the shoe about to explode her laces.

Even my husband noticed me jumping on the children for unimportant things and answering every request with an irritated voice and annoyed gesture. That evening we went for a drive, just Richard and I. It took me several hours of ranting and raving about how I never felt that my time was my own, and how I was sick to death of squabbling, injured children, before I figured out what was wrong. I rationalized that it was the new environment. (We were vacationing for a month in Jackson Hole, Wyoming.) For several weeks I'd been obsessed with packing, cleaning, and tying up loose ends on unreleased Church jobs. The night before the trip eight-year-old Josh had fallen off a fence and broken his arm, so we'd spent five valuable hours of packing time at the hospital. The morning we went to catch the plane, six-year-old Saydi had gotten her finger smashed in the van door, and two days after our arrival in Jackson, five-year-old Jonah had fallen out of the loft and lay on a bed for two days afraid to move for fear it would hurt.

*That must be the reason for my short temper and general irritation*, I thought, as I drove over to the other side of the mountain with Rick so that he could sign up for the annual tennis tournament.

As we walked into the racquet club in Jackson, however, the real cause for my irrational behavior suddenly came into focus. I unravelled it out loud on the way home, rattling off my frustrations nonstop to a poor, unsuspecting husband: "True, things have been hectic lately, but when I saw you walk into that racquet club *again*, I realized that I was angry because it seemed that you always—above everything else—have fun! You are always off to jog, off to fish, off to play tennis, and I am up to make breakfast, up to settle arguments and to clean the fridge, up to oversee practicing and make sure children's responsibilities are fulfilled. I feel physically sloggy and mentally drained."

Try as I might to blame someone else for all that, I could only come up with one person at fault: *me!* For several weeks I had neglected to have a good "Sunday Session" (see section 4 in chapter 3). I had sketched out a rough draft of the week with "Pack and Survive" as the vague heading, and had neglected to set any specific goals for myself or anyone else in the process.

Even more important than that, I felt, was the fact that I had been a physical zero for many months. I had rationalized that I was too busy to get involved in an exercise class and too tired to jog, and that surely running up and down stairs and lifting babies, boxes, and brooms was enough exercise. That frame of mind had become a bad habit.

Let me preface this next episode with the fact that I am not an athletic person. Even having been raised by the basketball star of Wyoming—best broad jumper, high jumper, mile runner (my mother)—didn't help. I abhorred baseball in the fourth grade because I was so hopelessly afraid that I was going to get hit in the face with a ball. I was always grateful when I got a bloody nose so I couldn't play. Basketball was even worse. I just couldn't get the rhythm of step, bounce, step, bounce.

For me, the thought of getting up to jog when I first became conscious in the morning seemed about as pleasant as putting a worm on a hook. Even with my acknowledged "unathleticness," however, I looked back over the last few years and realized that the times I had felt most happy, most excited about doing things with the kids, and most organized correlated with the times I had been taking yoga or aerobics classes or jogging.

Even though I knew physical fitness was important, I was putting everything else in first priority. In thinking my situation over carefully, I realized that mothers really have to put themselves first in order to get everything else running smoothly. Physical fitness is the key to many other things, no matter how painful it is in some of our cases.

The very next morning I dragged myself out of bed thinking, *Surely I can start this tomorrow; it looks so cold outside. In fact, it's actually snowing!* However, after the first hundred yards down the road with low clouds hanging in sheets around the Grand Tetons, and soft, big flecks brushing on my cheeks, and my lungs filling with clean, clear, cold air, as I listened to cattle mooing in the meadow, I wondered how I could ever have missed it. I felt my muscles perk up with unbelief—they were being used again and it felt wonderful!

*How can I fit that in?* I had asked myself the night before, and had realized that it was only another rationalization. *I am the master of my own fate.* Most husbands would be delighted to be asked to listen to or feed children for fifteen minutes before work while you clear out your cobwebs. If husbands aren't there, older children or a co-op system with a neighbor can be organized. Every person has her own level of need. Physical fitness, whether it be jogging or some other form of aerobics, is not only nice but essential to make you the best mother and wife you can be!

I returned home that morning and accepted egg on the carpet and cat food on the couch, the baby throwing food, and a black look from a child who doesn't like eggs—all with a smile and a determination to correct with a pleasant voice and control my temper regardless of the circumstances. Although obviously not a cure-all, it had already begun to help.

## Perils and Ponderings of Pregnancy

The best asset a pregnant woman can have is an understanding husband. Unfortunately, it took us several pregnancies to figure out that I very consistently said and did things during a pregnancy (especially in the first few months) which were very unusual. Besides crying when someone wins a car on "Let's Make a Deal," I get angry at almost everything. Now at the beginning of each pregnancy, when I start raving, the light dawns on my husband after a few brief episodes and he calls a family council.

The kids know about pregnancies right from the start, since they participate in the prayers about whether to have another child. Daddy sits me down on a chair and says to the "audience": "See this woman right here? She's your mother and she's about to be somebody else's mother! We all need to understand that when Mommy is pregnant she gets mad really easily and sometimes over things that don't deserve the attention. I'll tell you what to do when Mommy gets mad. Just put your arm around her and tell her you know she doesn't mean to be mean!" It doesn't always work that way, but it certainly helps. At least the kids can understand a little better and try to help!

When I get on my high horse with Richard and start making crazy, wild statements, he tries to put his arm around me and say, "I know you don't mean that!" Even though I always violently protest that I do mean it, I realize within a half-hour that I really don't, and it's forgotten.

Husbands, beware—and help! We need it!

Mother, don't expect too much of yourself during a pregnancy. Sometimes schedules have to slide for a while when you're too nauseated to get out of bed. But if your children have good habits and have been taught to take care of themselves, it's amazing how well things will go—without your strong arm.

If you fall asleep while you're reading stories to your three-year-old and are a grump during dinner, just remember—"this, too, will pass."

Diet is much more important during the child bearing and rearing years than at any other time in life. Not only does your body depend on it during that crucial time, but also the proper formation of another body is at stake.

The reading that I have done, especially in *Feed Your Kids Right*, by Lendon Smith, M.D. (New York: Dell, 1979), indicates that healthy children begin in the womb—that the physical health of a woman even before conception makes a marked difference in creating healthy children. Certainly there is no more important time to be concerned about and actually working on having a healthy body.

Often irritability or inability to cope with stressful situations is a direct result of not only hormonal imbalances but also vitamin or iron deficiences or the lack of proper exercise. Your body can easily be called your most valuable earthly possession. When something is wrong with it, everything else seems wrong. On the other hand, when you feel great there's nothing you can't do!

Although there are times when physical exercise is cut to a minimum because of a pregnancy or a new baby, don't rationalize your way back into the physical doldrums. Don't think you are sacrificing exercise and a good diet because you're too busy taking care of your family. It's hard to judge!

It's impossible to go into any more detail about exactly how much physical exercise is proper, especially during a pregnancy, because every body is so different. Some mothers stick to tennis, aerobics, or the Jane Fonda Exercise in Pregnancy program right up to the delivery day. Others may have to go to bed for nine months to save the baby. Check with your doctor and use your own good sense in knowing what is best for you.

Don't make the mistake of thinking you must eat for two during a pregnancy, and end up the size of two after your baby is delivered. Neither should you starve yourself to death so that you can have your "model's" figure back two weeks after delivery.

Again, you need to analyze your own body, your metabolism, and your needs, and then come up with a plan to maintain it at a satisfying level, so that when the pregnancy is over, you don't have to feel depressed about looking terrible and struggling to lose fifteen pounds while you're nursing a baby. An ounce of prevention *is* worth a pound of cure!

CHALLENGES

1. Remember that your irritability level often has to do with your diet and exercise. Put yourself first for the benefit of everyone else in your family and stick to a good physical fitness program and diet.

2. Don't expect too much of yourself during pregnancy, but do take fastidious care of your body. Diet, exercise, and feeling good about yourself are crucial! (Don't worry about your feet; they're still there, you just can't see them for a while.)

---

## 10. Be Flexible

Now that we have gone through a long list of fairly specific things that a mother can do to cope with stress, I cannot close without stating what may seem to be the antithesis of many of the things we've just discussed: Be flexible!

An article in the *Washington Post* told of a woman who had wanted to survey families firsthand to find whether there was a common thread in well-adjusted families as well as in the unhappy ones. In order to feel that her study had some depth, she decided to actually live with each family for a period of one month. Her survey involved twenty families from all different social and economic levels. Many of her findings were vague because she found each family to be so different. But one thing that she could single out as a common characteristic of the happiest families was that they were "flexible."

The columnist didn't explain herself in great detail, but did indicate that flexibility did not mean that members of the family were not high achievers, only that when situations arose that required things to happen at a different time or place, the changes occurred without a great deal of fuss.

Being flexible doesn't mean eliminating goals or plans when they aren't convenient. It simply means finding a better time to do them (or if not better, at least more convenient). It also means facing the reality that sometimes, instead of doing something a few hours or days or even years later, you might have to accomplish your goal in an entirely different way.

Flexibility may mean putting away the material you bought to make Christmas clothes until Valentine's Day or next Christmas. Sometimes it may even mean putting on the top shelf until your children are older a hobby or a career you love. It may mean that an intense daily schedule that really works must be relaxed because of morning sickness or the arrival of a new baby. Once in a while it means taking the kids to church with two heads unwashed and one set of unmatched socks. It may mean dropping some parsley around a plate of Jell-o that dropped out of its mold like a glob of wet plaster of Paris on the day of your special luncheon and saying to yourself, "Never mind, they'll never know what it should have looked like anyway." It may even mean giving up a wonderful vacation that you've planned on for months, because of a family illness or death.

Situations arise every day that require us to decide whether we're going to be flexible. Sometimes we realize that we can fit in taking a meal to an unexpectedly sick friend on an already hectic day. Sometimes flexibility requires us to realize that someone else could truly help a friend in need better than we could, even though we'd rather do it ourselves.

One of a mother's great keys to flexibility is the use of lateral thinking—a thought process advocated by Edward de Bono, born in Malta and educated at Oxford and Cambridge Universities. He tells a story of a merchant's daughter to illustrate lateral thinking. It seems that the merchant had the misfortune of owing a large sum to a ruthless creditor. The old and ugly creditor fancied the merchant's beautiful daughter and said he would cancel the debt if he could have the girl instead.

Seeing that the daughter was horrified at the proposal, the creditor proposed that they let providence decide the matter. He picked up two pebbles from the pebble-strewn path, put them in his hat, and told the girl that if she drew the white pebble he would release the debt and leave them alone. If she drew the black pebble, however, she would have to go with him. The girl, sharp-eyed with fright, saw that he had put two black pebbles into his hat.

She employed lateral thinking. She pulled a pebble from the hat, and without looking at it fumbled and dropped it to the path, where it was quickly lost among the other pebbles. "Oh, how clumsy of me," she said, "but never mind, if you look into the hat you will be able to tell which pebble I chose by the color of the one that is left." (*The Use of Lateral Thinking*, Harmondworth, Middlesex, England: Penguin Books, 1971.)

*Our* dilemmas may be not quite as dire as the one cited here, but still "catch-22" type situations face us constantly as mothers. Use your mental effort to think laterally and produce a creative solution.

Lateral thinking is a careful thought process that helps us to be flexible and to get things done in a way we wouldn't have thought of through normal direct reasoning. One simple, everyday example in my life occurred on an airplane one day. Richard had been really excited about a new paperback novel he was reading and was anxious to have me read it so that we could talk about it. As I rummaged through my bag to find it while the stewardess began her "how-to-fasten-your-seatbelt" procedure he said, "Where's my book? I'm at an exciting part."

"Hey, I thought this was my chance to catch up with you," I pleaded. He looked at my face as I handed him the book, thought silently for about fifteen seconds, then with a smile he gallantly tore the book in halves and handed me the first half. Although it took the man across the aisle a few minutes to recover, I smiled too and wished I had thought of it first.

CHALLENGES

1. Use lateral thinking to take a different, easier "route" to the desired end, especially when you think you've got more to do than you can handle.

2. Throw over the routine once in a while and do something crazy. Go to a midnight movie with your husband even though there's school tomorrow. Take the kids to get ice cream in their pajamas. Let your children know that you like to be crazy too. Sleep out with them on the lawn once in a while. Drop everything and go on a spur-of-the-moment vacation for a couple of days—even if it's hard to rearrange and leave responsibilities and pack everybody up.

Everybody needs a break once in a while. Sleep in on Saturday morning even though you've got "thousands" of things to do. Serve hot dogs for Sunday dinner. Be flexible!

# Chapter Five

# Children Are Individuals

*B*eing far away from the hairdresser I knew and trusted, and having whacked away a few hunks of hair myself without success, I finally called a friend and asked her to recommend someone who could cut my hair. I seldom worry about haircuts, but occasionally the situation arises when the "mop" gets unbearable; it seems to coincide with needing to look nice for a special occasion.

I called for an appointment on the only day I could arrange for a baby sitter, only to find that that particular girl was off duty. The receptionist assured me, however, that Leetsa would do a beautiful job. When I arrived, with memories of past unhappy experiences, I carefully pointed out to Leetsa pictures of hair I liked, and strongly indicated that that was what I wanted. Carefully I explained that my husband had great fears about "scissor-happy" haircutters, and all the while she smiled and said in her very Greek accent, "I will do you a beautiful job!"

She took scissors in hand and started snipping. I tried not to gasp when I saw her cut the first chunk out of the side of my hair. I calmly suggested that it should perhaps be a little longer, but the smile remained and I'll probably never know how much she had understood about what I wanted. She snipped and sheared and kept talking in her broken English about how useful it was to have twenty years of experience. "I don' like it when people don' like to try things new," she chattered. "Oh, you have such lovely hair!"

I inwardly shrugged my shoulders and decided that there was really nothing I could do, so I drifted off into my own thoughts as the hair showered down around me. "This woman," I thought, "has not heard one thing I've said. She took one look at me and decided how she thought I would look best, and indeed, under her 'skilled' scissors, that is the way I will look, like it or not."

Having just had a discussion with one of our older girls about what was "cute" and what wasn't, I realized that this woman was like many mothers! They refuse to let their children be individuals because they have their own ideas about what they would like those children to be, do, look, and wear! Each child is a spectacular individual, desperate to be himself from the moment he bursts forth in the delivery room.

How well we help our children to be individuals—the kind they want to be—really depends on us, on how well we can guide them in the right direction without being pushy, and offer suggestions without being tyrannical.

Children are not like lumps of clay that we can form into any shape we desire. They are much more like seeds. The fruit is already in the kernel. It is our responsibility to water and nurture and prune and give sunlight to that little individual, so that he can become the beautiful plant he was intended to be.

The two most important skills in producing terrific individuals are: first, our ability to listen with our minds and hearts and our very souls to what each child wants and needs to become; and second, our ability to observe, to perceive talents and needs by watching our children.

I was brought back to real life from my daydreams as Leetsa stuck a large mirror in my hand and beamed at me over my shorn locks. To my amazement my hair looked just like hers, except that hers was blond. It was all I could do to keep from giggling as she exclaimed over how lovely I looked and said that this was just the perfect haircut for me.

I tried to be honest and told her I had learned some very interesting things from having watched her cut my hair. She blindly took it as a great compliment and I left, weighing a pound or two lighter. But I realized that, while it would take me six months to begin to look normal again, some children *never* recover from a strong-willed, highly opinionated mother who thinks she always knows what's best for her child and unwittingly makes the child into "herself," whether intentionally or not.

Let's look into some specific methods for raising individuals:

---

## Mommy Dates

As many mothers do, we call the time I spend alone with an individual child a "mommy date." These dates range from the well-planned, elaborate kind to the ridiculously simple, spur-of-the-moment kind. As more children have joined our family I have found it hard to spend long lengths of time with each child each week, and a good mommy date has sometimes consisted of grabbing a six-year-old's hand on the way out the door to the grocery store with a "Come on, let's talk" look in my eye.

The challenge on that kind of "date" is getting the grocery list off my mind and turning my attention to the child. Most mommy dates are good; some are disastrous (the kind when you end up yelling at the child because he's bothering you when you're trying to decide whether or not to buy something)—but there are a few I can remember with each child that were truly great! One such event I remember well, because I recorded it in my journal right after we returned home:

It was a cold, crisp, autumn morning when I took my first real walk in the English countryside. The purpose was a mommy date, and my companion was Joshua—just three years old—our first little son.

With two little fingers in my hand (he liked it that way) we walked along the bridle path that begins across the street from our house and winds its way through beautiful trees, vegetation, and stately estates with expensive cars parked in front of lush gardens obviously kept by meticulous gardeners.

Our first discovery was round, red autumn berries, which Joshua, "the great observer," carried in his hot little hand almost all the way back home before he finally gave in to the urge and squashed them.

Almost immediately we encountered one nice, big, lovable, friendly dog who, for some unknown reason, was in a hurry to get home and didn't stop long to talk—and one large, white, manicured French poodle who stared motionless at us until we got to within three feet. We stopped and then I said, "Hi, dog!" He gave two ferocious barks and ran in the other direction. This startled me as much as it did Josh and I realized as it happened that I grasped his hand just as tightly as he did mine.

On we went, and the silence was broken only by birds tweetering in the huge, dense trees overhead and a curious little boy saying (at about fifteen-second intervals) "What's daaaaaat?" —intermingled with "We—are—on—a—mommy—date" in his sweet little robot voice. He especially liked the hoofprints in the mud and took time to mention each one.

As we walked along the path we saw crowds and crowds of ivy with small green-of-a-different-color growths on the end of each shoot, many six or eight inches long—all grown the past week. The long-awaited rain had produced almost the same result as hot oil on popcorn. The earth had been so thirsty for so long—as we had just come to the end of a summer-long drought —and evidences of the joy of the week-long nourishment were evident everywhere.

It was a true "seldom day," the first day we'd "seen our breath" in England, and as we slowly passed by the stables and each footprint, I could feel a little boy's sense of individuality as he chose the way to go and the things to talk about.

Just as we rounded the corner onto the "civilized" road again, both Mum and son were delighted to see a big lorry (we call them trucks) parked on the sidewalk, six inches from a tall wood fence and next to a quaint old barn. Directly over the fence lay a huge stack of wet straw smouldering—no, steaming— in the frosty morning air.

To our delight the truck driver got out, went to the back of the truck, and began to operate a huge hydraulic lift connected to a gruesome-looking clawlike apparatus that picked up the straw in a huge clump on the other side of the fence and promptly dumped it into the back of the truck. We first moved closer to get a better look, but the noise was deafening, and Josh carefully and deliberately backed up about ten or twenty feet, stopped, and every minute or so reassured himself by saying, "It won't hurt me!" Every time I asked if he wanted to go home or go closer he replied with conviction, "I want to stay right here!"

At last, after a long study of the subject, he decided he was ready to proceed and we wound our way back down the path-roads which I now recognized—still finding treasures to add to our collection, to show the girls at home.

The sunshine broke through and we finished our date with a wave at the milkman, a small white feather, a large gray feather, four uncrushable berries off a nearby tree, a better knowledge of what was green and what was red, three mushrooms with soft, slated undersides, and one yellow flower.

An unforgettable morning!

Although almost every mommy date is time well spent, some are more productive than others. Sometimes we have double dates, which is also kind of fun if you have more than two children. To observe how different pairs relate to you and each other is very interesting.

If you think you have to plan a big trip with each child, you'll probably end up doing nothing. Keep it simple and plan something big once a month or so. Schedule the other dates into your plan each Sunday and you'll find yourself being much more consistent. Don't feel guilty about combining a mommy date with an errand. Probably our little children's favorite spot for a mommy date is the grocery store.

Watch your child meticulously. Some children are better than others at telling you that they need extra time alone with you. One day one of our little girls came to me and said, "Mom, I feel depribed." Further investigation revealed that she felt she had been skipped on her turn for a mommy date, and in looking back we realized that she was right. Unexpected things kept popping up just at her moment to go.

When all is said and done, the most important part of mothering is having a good, productive relationship with each child as an individual. This is also the hardest part when you have more than one little child. Some things are just impossible to teach to "the mobs" all at once. Divide and conquer!

## Look at the World Through His Eyes

Take time to sit back and think about one child at a time. Look at the world through his eyes for a few minutes. Daydream yourself into his desk at school. Think about how he relates to his friends and his teacher. This is a hard mental exercise, but if you stick to it for a few minutes you will begin to realize why he is the way he is. Visualize how his personality is fitting in with his surroundings, and think what you can do to help. Do something special just for him.

It is so easy for a little child to get lost in the crowd. I often think of the story of the little boy who was pounding on his mother's leg and trying to get her attention amidst the hectic preparations for dinner so he could show her a bruise on his finger. Finally, after his repeated attempts, the mother stopped and, impatient with the interruption, said, "Well, honey, I can't do anything about it, can I?"

"Yes, Mommy," her little son said in an exasperated voice. "You could have said 'Oh.' " Sometimes all a child needs is a little sympathy.

One other thing to try as you look through your child's eyes is to ask him how he thinks you can improve. I've gotten some of my best self-improvement ideas from the suggestions of the kids. Some things are predictable and some aren't; some are hilarious and some are dead serious—but they've all been helpful.

## Empty Books

Years ago, when our first two little girls were tiny, a friend suggested something for which I will always be grateful. It involved buying what we call "empty books"—bound books with blank pages. At the birth of each child I start a new book just for him. I record the "gory" details of the wild ride to the hospital, and also the great joy we felt at having that little individual join our family. From then on, every few months I record his progress, write about special events, and slip in a picture or two to remind me about how he looked just then, even though at the moment I think I'll never forget. I write in the first person, like a long letter to the child from me.

The children know that I'm keeping their books, but they will not be allowed to see them until their wedding days. Even though it's hard to find time to write (I use my time on my "getaways" to catch up), and I usually only make entries about every six months, those books are some of our most precious belongings.

This activity helps me to see the world through each child's eyes and to make myself think about him or her as an individual. Already I look back at the childhood of my older children and realize that I would have forgotten those special moments if I hadn't recorded them.

---

## Set Goals for Them and With Them

I like to use some time at the beginning of each season to re-evaluate each child and his or her gifts and interests to see how they can be used to the maximum. I set goals in my mind for each child, and at least one goal to do something with him or her (read a book, sew a pillow, and so on).

Then, with these goals in mind, I go home and discuss with each child in his Sunday Session what gifts I think he has and what I think we should do to maximize them. When those dreams are turned into actual step-by-step goals on paper, the process gets exciting.

I like to post my goals for the children somewhere I will be certain to look once a week, so I don't forget them. I also have to take into account the fact that sometimes the kids have no interest in "my" goals, so we opt for theirs and wait. (Sometimes things come to those who wait.)

## Music Lessons and Other Trials

The last time the piano tuner came to work on our lovely, relatively new piano, he found a set of rhythm sticks, a pair of tweezers, a small doll, a bar of soap, and a pinewood derby inside. In utter amazement he looked at me and said seriously, "Your children don't play the piano, they play in the piano." So goes our life.

Music has been a big part of my life ever since I can remember. Actually, I guess I was involved even before that, because I come from a long line of musicians on both sides of the family. Besides having taught school for about forty-eight years, my mother spent much of her early life playing piano by ear in an old-time Saturday night dance band with her father and his fiddle. Her formal music education followed, and has brought immeasurable joy to the lives of about thirty piano students "on the side" every year for the past fifty-five years—and probably will do so for another twenty years (she's only seventy-seven).

I used to hate those cold mornings up at Bear Lake— bundling up in Mom's old beaver coat and practicing first on piano and then violin (or vice versa) while my sister practiced the other. I remember longing to be a normal child who could just get up, eat breakfast, and go to school, and then come home afterward and watch "Leave It to Beaver." There was none of that for us! There was no playing with friends, no TV, no after-school get-togethers before our practicing was done.

I can still remember mother standing over me with a clenched fist, watching the tears of frustration roll down my cheeks, and saying, "Someday you'll thank me for this." She was right! I thank her in my heart almost daily when I think of the fun I'd be missing if she hadn't made me become a musician— whether I liked it or not.

Now I face the same dilemma with my children. After the first few years of struggling to get our oldest daughter to practice, I remembered what had taken the sting out of practicing for us (my sister and me). From the time we were eight, our parents expected us to earn our own money for treats, movies, *and* clothes. They provided us with a way of doing that by paying us to

practice. The pay was very meager, but if we had a perfect practice record at the end of the week, our money was doubled.

Richard and I wondered why we hadn't thought of it sooner.
A system was devised and our first two little practicers changed
from whining woefuls to eager earners. We gave them their own
alarm clocks and turned the responsibility over to them for
getting started on time to finish by breakfast time.

Not only was there a complete about-face in their attitude
toward practicing, but they also were thrilled about buying
clothes with their very own money. Those clothes were suddenly
put on hangers and taken care of meticulously because their
owners had worked hard to buy them. (It takes about a month
to earn enough for a dress.)

We still buy Christmas and birthday clothes and underwear
(I hate to think what the "undies" would look like if the children
decided when to buy them), and there are still complaints here
and there, but for the most part everybody's happy.

I address the subject of music lessons or any kind of lessons
cautiously because children are so different. Parents are usually
too decisive or too indecisive, and teachers are as different as
night and day.

How soon your child should begin lessons depends on how
perceptive you are to his natural ability, the time you have to
commit, and the teachers available. A good teacher can change
your child's life, increase his love for music, and teach him self-
discipline—a pretty impressive contribution. A poor teacher can
squelch his interest and give him a bad taste in his mouth for
music—pretty scary. Parents can push too much or not enough.
Often we have to depend on intuition and inspiration to get us
through the hard decisions.

Some teachers are wonderful for some children and devas-
tating to others. Don't be afraid to have a long chat with a pros-
pective teacher to learn about his philosophy of teaching. Some
are geared to making students professionals. Others are more
interested in nurturing a love for music as a discipline and source
of enjoyment. Decide what you really think is best for your child

and then stick to it tenaciously. Someday he'll thank you for that.

Our music situation may be different from most. Because I was a music education major, I teach the children myself. I admit that there are advantages and disadvantages to that. They don't practice with the "fear-of-teacher-condemnation" in mind as much as they would otherwise, and it takes extra time and organization on my part. On the other hand, however, it saves hours and hours of running kids back and forth to music lessons, and I use that time to expose them to other lessons in fields in which I have no expertise.

Through it all I have gained a great respect for the value of teaching your own children *something.* Use your expertise and pass it on to your children—whether it involves teaching them how to read, how to cook, or how to knit (boys, too). I'm convinced that you can know your children much better if you understand how they learn.

In teaching my children music, for instance, I have realized that it's much harder for our more artistic children to learn to read notes. I'm amazed at how much easier it is for the calculative, mathematical types to learn notes and to sightread quickly. On the other hand, the "soul" that comes out of the artistic child is heartwarming.

There can't be a better way to get to know your child as an individual. It is very interesting to see how each child tackles a problem, handles frustration, and reacts to triumph.

This year our family is "majoring" in education (each year we try to establish a major and a minor to work on as a family). Each child at some time during the year (not all at once) is taking a class on his or her special interest. On Fridays at dinner they report what they learned that week, so as to "educate" the other children (parents too) in their various fields.

It is important to expose your children to as many things as you can—from gymnastics to ballet, from computer programming to dramatics—but remember that there is only one of you and twenty-four hours in a day. Whether they realize it or not, the kids would rather have a happy mother at home with them in the afternoons once in a while than all the art lessons in the world.

Some years will be harder than others. Many sacrifices must be made—especially if you have a child who does want to make ballet or music a career. There may be a point in life when one of these interests becomes all-consuming. Until that happens, however, our job as mothers is to try to expose our children to as many of the wonderful things in life as we can so that they can have a broad base from which to choose.

Since I know music best, I must conclude by saying that studying music is an excellent learning process and a tool for self-discipline, whether your child is tremendously talented or not. (How far you go has to be between you and the child as an individual.) One of our greatest joys as a family (though it wasn't always this way) is being able to start each morning right at 6:30 with a hymn played by our family string quartet. I can honestly say that—even now—it's worth all the blood, sweat, and tears!

CHALLENGES

1. Arrange for some kind of a mommy date for each child every couple of weeks. Every one does not need to be long and elaborate. Sometimes just a few minutes alone with each child can do wonders. Plan it into your Sunday Session so you know exactly when it will happen. If you fail here and there, don't get the "failure syndrome." Do better next week.

2. Try spending a few minutes at least once a month concentrating on looking at the world through one particular child's eyes. Think about how he must feel about his siblings, his teachers, his responsibilities, his parents. Use the empathy you feel to handle that child more skillfully—especially during times of stress.

3. Get an "empty book" for each child and try just writing your observations of him every few months. Even if you're years behind on some, something from there on up is better than nothing at all!

4. Set goals *for* your children according to your best assessment of their gifts and needs, and set goals *with* them according to their best understanding of themselves. Help them to achieve by checking their progress each Sunday.

5. Involve your child with some kind of lessons to develop self-discipline and self-confidence. Music is an excellent medium but is not the only way to learn these great principles. Skiing, swimming, soccer, or even chess can accomplish many of the same things. Let these skills help you learn things about your child. Whatever skills are chosen, let the children know that you expect their *best!*

# Chapter 6

# A Joyful Partnership

W e've talked a lot about dealing with children, but we can't leave the topic of motherhood without saying a few words about husbands. The most joyful mothers are generally joyful partners as well.

## What to Do With a Husband

In those glowing days of your courtship with a person you hardly knew but loved, it was hard to imagine ever having to work at a good relationship with each other. That man in your life occupied 95 percent of your thought and concentration.

As the years of marriage pass, the deciding factor as to whether or not the relationship becomes more meaningful, more deep and full, rewarding, intriguing, and yes, even more fun, can be stated in one word: communication!

Good, open, positive communication takes effort, love, care, and courage. Sometimes with the distractions of earning a living, keeping up a home, and having and raising children, it seems much easier to run like two trains along parallel tracks—each speeding along, doing its own thing well, but never touching or crossing paths with the other.

We've all experienced difficult times. For example, when you've just been through a traumatic delivery of a new baby and are trying to cope with nursing, filling baby's needs, and getting your body back together, your husband may lean over you as you nod off to sleep, nursing the baby in the rocking chair, and say, "Hi, remember me?"

If these hard times are handled sensitively by both partners, however, they can be occasions of communication and of letting love grow brighter.

Before we were married I never dreamed that Richard would eat in bed and floss his teeth every time there was a moment of silence, change the TV station at every advertisement, and be late for almost every meal. I know his idiosyncrasies well by now, and despite all of them it is easy for me to say that I love him much more than I did on our wedding day. Our relationship has become immeasurably more deep and meaningful.

I attribute much of this to the fact that he taught me to communicate. This was not an easy job! I grew up with the idea that if something bothered you or made you angry you should try to be nice and not tell anybody. Richard changed all that. He taught me so well how to express my feelings that I'm sure that he often wishes he had never done it.

Communicating began on day one of our relationship. We are both very strong willed, and almost every day brought out some sort of battle of the wills. In fact, we did not stay out until three in the morning for the same reason many people do while dating; we were out there having good, rousing arguments! To this day we enjoy nice "heated" discussions. We always get the problem resolved, and I guess in the back of our minds we argue partly because it's so much fun to make up! (The funny thing is that I can't remember for the life of me what any of those arguments were about.)

It was never difficult for me to hold up my end of the case in a "discussion." The hard part was communicating my feelings when I felt hurt or unappreciated or overworked. I preferred to just suffer in silence and let the bad feeling fester until it popped out in unexpected ways. For example, I would get furious because Richard was still out skiing when he was supposed to be home for dinner, when what I was really mad about was that I wasn't organizing my time well enough to get to the slopes myself!

We have decided that the old saying: "Some things are better left unsaid," is true in every relationship except a marriage. (Of course, there is a right and a wrong way to say everything.)

If your husband is never sure how you feel about his job, your happiness level, or his needs, it makes him feel very in-

secure. Tell him exactly how you feel and you will feel the
barriers in your marriage—if they're beginning to rise—start to
crumble. It's not easy. Sometimes it takes days or months to
work out, but it's the most valuable thing you can do to improve
your marriage.

Following are five specific methods of communication that
help greatly to create a really productive partnership.

1. *Do window deeds.* At the beginning of our marriage we
decided to each think of at least one thoughtful deed per week to
do for the other. (I plan mine during my Sunday Session.) The
deed shows that we are looking through a "window" to see the
needs of the other person instead of having everything seem like
a mirror that reflects our own needs.

Most window deeds are small (during some hectic weeks
they're almost unrecognizable) but every one is appreciated and
needed. Sometimes the deed might simply be your preparing him
a *real* dinner for a change, instead of just kids' fare. My husband
loves gourmet food. It means a lot to him if I fix him an arti-
choke and crack open a bottle of Perrier water when we get a
chance to settle down to a quiet evening together after the
"tribe" is tucked in.

One smart young mother said that she had realized how
often her husband was doing things that she really needed but
failed to thank him for. She went right out and made a big sign
and posted it above the garbage cans in the garage. It said,
"Thanks for always taking out the garbage!" "He liked it so
much that it's still there," she smiled.

As big and strong and tough as they are, husbands need a
lot of sympathy and tender loving care. When you have gone
through several pregnancies and deliveries and all the discomforts and pain involved, it's hard to be too sympathetic about a
sprained arm that keeps your husband from eating, drinking, or
smiling on his own. Often a bad cold will send him straight to
bed for three days. (That reminds me of how embarrassed I was
one day when I had had an unusually wild day and a bad cold.
As I settled into the dentist's chair, he took one look at me, felt
my forehead, told me that I was sick and had a fever, and that I

was to go straight home to bed. He wouldn't even do my teeth! I did the afternoon car-pool anyway.)

It always kind of tickles me to wake up in the morning to a scruffy-looking, groggy guy who says, "I guess you realize that I didn't sleep one wink last night! I had *such* a sore toe!" I used to kind of roll my eyes and giggle, but now I try to be really sympathetic and understanding and try to nurse him back to health. It does wonders for his feeling of well-being and that leftover need to be mothered.

More than anything in the world my husband loves me to rub his feet! (I can't think of anything more disgusting.) He thinks it's the answer to releasing all the tension in every part of his body. My ultimate Christmas gift to him was coupons for foot rubs. It meant even more to him knowing that I was not particularly fond of the task.

It's easy to get priorities mixed up. When we are laden with children's needs, household responsibilities, and social demands, it's crucial to remember that our first priority in the love and care of others should be our husbands!

I have a good friend with five little children whose husband walked off with another girl one day and never came back. She confided in me: "If only I could take back those days when my husband came home from a hard day's work and I brushed by him thinking, 'I don't have time for you, I'm too busy being a good mother'!"

Our husbands need us to hold up our end of the partnership by showing them how much we love and appreciate them. On your husband's next birthday, try writing a "spouse description." Include your feelings about him emotionally, socially, physically, and mentally. Maybe you'll realize some things that even you didn't know.

2. *Have five-facet reviews.* Communicate about the children in a meaningful way. Take one evening a month to get away together and talk about each child as an individual. Don't just reminisce over the cute things they say and do; really zero in on each individual. Actually take notes and talk about each one of them (1) physically, (2) socially, (3) emotionally, (4) mentally, and

(5) spiritually. This is a wonderful mental exercise. You will realize that you know more about your children than you thought you did. It's extremely helpful for your husband to get your perspective because you are with them more than he is.

One end result will be a heightening of your appreciation of many things about your children. The most valuable result, however, is being able to come up with some possible solutions for some of their problems so that you can work on them as a team during the month ahead.

3. *Share goals and dreams.* It's hard to get anywhere in a marriage if you don't know where you're going. Once a year, usually at the start of the new year, Richard and I find a lot of satisfaction in going over our long-range goals. We plan what we'd like to have accomplished in five years—where we might be and what everybody might be like. It's fun to try to visualize what each child will be like in five years, and horrifying to realize how old *we'll* be.

When we've taken a stab at what we'd like things to be like in five years, both as a partnership and individually, we try to translate that down into one-year goals. In September we plan the family's "major and minor" subjects for concentration that year, and in the spring we talk about what we'd like to accomplish during the summer.

There's nothing more exhilarating than really planning together! We've learned to love the concept of synergism, which states that the whole is greater than the sum of its parts (or 2 + 2 = 5). We find that each of us standing alone can't really do much, but when we combine our efforts, the result is much greater.

4. *Discover executive sessions and nightly planning.* Usually on Sunday nights after we have our individual Sunday Sessions and our "adult meeting" with the kids, we have what we call the "executive session." At the first of the month this session involves planning or sketching out the month; at the beginning of each week, the week. We decide together what "joys" and "responsibilities" we're working on with the children (refer to

*Teaching Children Joy* and *Teaching Children Respon*
details) and what word we're concentrating on as a cou
have a group of favorite words that mean a lot to us—
teristics we try to work into our week's thought and action.)

Sometimes the session includes a financial discussion and
always try to end with an eyeball-to-eyeball, one-at-a-time verba-
ization about how we feel about life at the moment and especially about each other.

At particularly hectic times (it works better if you do it all
the time) we do nightly planning together. Just before we kneel
down together each night we take two pieces of paper with a
piece of carbon paper between and a line drawn down the
middle. He writes his schedule for the next day on one side and I
write mine on the other. It's wonderful to be able to know where
he is when I need him, and vice versa.

5. *Make your marriage a three-way partnership.* Nothing is
more important for a couple than to realize that they can do
nothing without the Lord's help. Richard and I appreciate the
opportunity to kneel together each night and pour out our
appreciation to him. When we were first married, it seemed that
I always worried because Richard forgot to bless somebody or I
forgot his mother, so we decided on a new plan, which we've
used ever since. One of us, let us say it is Richard, begins the
prayer. When he is finished with all he has to say, he squeezes
my hand and I take over with the thoughts of my heart and then
conclude the prayer. After that we have a few minutes of silent,
individual prayer.

It is wonderful to feel that we have a real partnership with
our Heavenly Father, and to realize both that there is nothing
we can do without him, and nothing we can't do with him!

## What to Do With a Part-time Husband

Because of the heavy responsibilities of Church callings or
full-time jobs that require lots of traveling or after-hours work,
many of us live for long periods with part-time husbands. We

have probably all felt at some time or other the thoughts so well expressed in this poem by Cathy C. Peterson, which I use with permission.

### Sunday and Pregnant

Bold-bellied
Baggy-eyed
Kiddies calling
Patience tried.
   Aching back
   Aching head
   Facing Sunday
   Doom and dread.
      Running noses
      Chronic wiper
      Constant wringing
      Dirty diaper.
         Daddy's meetings—
         Gone all day
         Try to study (?)
         Try to pray (?)
   Sabbath, Sabbath
   Day of Rest
   Keeping sane
   Is Sunday's test!

There have been periods when Richard has had to travel enough that I have had a good taste of "survival practice." And I've spent long hours with other wives who have been without their husbands for months at a time, or had them only on weekends, or had husbands in Church callings that always took them away on weekends. Here is what I've learned:

1. Being consistent about all five steps just mentioned is even more important when responsibilities outside the home keep the husband away. In fact, the need probably doubles although the time is often halved. Plan carefully!

2. Make the best possible use of the time he is at home. If he is often only home on weekends, get your house clean and all the nitty-gritties done during the week so that you can have some fun as a family or as a couple while he's there.

3. Learn to be flexible. I know that one of the biggest frustrations of having a part-time husband is that you get going on your plan for the week and then he pops in and needs to change everything. (Oops, lack of planning again—but it happens.) Both partners need to be flexible on this sort of thing.

4. Learn to be independent. Don't sit home and cry because the kitchen sink needs unplugging and the garbage has to be taken out. Take matters into your own hands and do it or get someone else to do it. Your husband will have other things to do when he gets there besides work on your list of repairs.

5. Communicate! Don't sit and mourn for yourself because you feel overworked, underpaid, and unappreciated. Let him know exactly how you feel. Be a true partner and let him know your frustrations. (Try to be kind.) If he's willing to work on the partnership too, and realizes that you are his first priority, he'll sit up and listen and help work out some ways to make it easier for you both.

---

## What to Do Without a Husband

I wish I could be more help to you single mothers. When you lose a husband through divorce or death your job is doubled! Besides the obvious feelings of hurt and loss, you also oftentimes have to become the breadwinners.

Often friends or family have to fill in as partners. Probably what you need most is someone to talk to, to help you with decisions and frustrations. Although this is the ideal, you also must realize that even though there are usually people to give help and advice, you can't always plan on it. The greatest key must be learning to be independent, to grow and to change and to act as though everything depended on you—because it does.

Although this is the hardest problem I can visualize as a mother, just like everything else it can destroy you or make you become better.

A friend of ours who had lost a child said after the initial shock was over and life began to resume, "It really doesn't matter what happens to you in life, only how you handle it." Even in the face of this hardest of all challenges, you can be a "joyful mother."

CHALLENGES

1. Try concentrating on doing something special for your husband as a first-priority item every week for one month. If he doesn't notice, tell him you're doing it and keep at it. He may even decide to do the same for you.

2. Faithfully have "five-facet reviews" with your husband once a month for three months, and see if these don't improve not only your children but your ability to work together as partners on a common goal! Dream together as a couple and as a family. Set long-range objectives. Refer to them often. Plan together nightly so that you know each other's schedules and problems daily. Be sure that you include your Heavenly Father as the "managing partner" in the three-way partnership of your life.

3. When your husband is traveling and away frequently it is even more important to communicate with him and use the time wisely while he is home. Learn to be flexible, and ask him to do the same. Oftentimes he must realize that *he* has to fit into your schedule, not always vice versa. Learn to be independent, but when you are upset about his long or frequent absences tell him about it. Many times it just doesn't *have* to be that way. Don't let resentment and other bad feelings boil inside until time settles them to a "simmer." Communicate, communicate, communicate! Especially when it's hard. You cannot create a true oneness in marriage unless you know exactly how your partner feels and you let him know exactly how you feel.

4. If you have lost your partner, communicate with friends and loved ones. Use a journal to write your feelings. Thoughts and solutions may pop out that you did not know were inside of you.

# Chapter 7

# Love the Present

Oe beautiful autumn morning I was working on this book in my car, which was parked at a rest area on a narrow canyon road ablaze with the golds, reds, and yellows of fall. I looked up and noticed that most of the traffic going by was made up of stunning antique autos from the era of the early 1900s—all with numbers on the back and obviously ready for some sort of car rally somewhere up the road.

Being a lover of old cars, I found myself looking up to smile and admire every time one passed by. As the procession went on, I couldn't help but notice that the people in the cars were mostly old people—ladies with gray hair pulled back in buns and scarves, men in top hats, with red handkerchieves tied around their necks. Many were in open-air cars with flawless paint jobs; some were in rumble seats and most were sitting forward in their seats, obviously drinking in the joy of the moment: the breathtaking sights and sounds and smells of autumn. All were smiling. Many honked horns and waved at anything and everything in sight (mostly leaves and rocks). They were having the time of their lives!

"How wonderful it would be," I thought, "to enjoy every day like that!" My mind quickly reverted back to a conversation I'd had with Richard just the night before:

I was depressed. The kitchen had been being remodeled for about two and one-half months, but the metal trim had never been installed in the doorway so the linoleum was getting torn. The wallpaper had been sitting in the basement for two weeks waiting for somebody to put it up. (Having come to the end of our remodeling budget I decided it had to be me.)

The kids were all adjusting to a new year at school. Our shy junior-high student was miserable trying to cope with being the worst player on the soccer team. Another child needed to be told to unload the dishwasher (or do anything else, for that matter) at least eight times before it got done. Our kindergartner whined from 11:30 when he got home from school until bedtime. The three-year-old had just hit the "terrible twos" a year late. Our fifth-grader had banged her head on a brick wall in a P.E. class and had complained of headaches for days. The second-grader begged nonstop for friends to come over, and the baby's latest hobby was consistently messing his diaper while he was in bed and then taking the diaper off and spreading a thin coat all over the sheets, the walls, and his body. (No amount of pleading, coaxing, explaining, or spanking could change his mind.)

That, along with trying to squeeze in haircuts, birthday parties, school activities, tulip planting, children's lessons, church meetings, and Cub Scouts made me feel absolutely depressed!

"Now, wait a minute!" Richard said with a smile, in his usual down-to-earth-I've-got-a-solution-for-this-problem way. "Step back and look at yourself for a minute. You have the new kitchen you've always wanted, seven terrific kids, and a *wonderful* husband. Don't live in the past or the future. Enjoy the present—even if it's hard."

He was absolutely right. For everything that was wrong or inconvenient, I could, if I tried, think of several things that were wonderful. It's easy to live for the future: "Won't it be lovely when the baby can walk and I don't have to carry him everywhere," or for the past: "Wasn't it lovely when the baby just sat in one place and couldn't pull everything out of the cupboards or get lost!"

No matter what is happening in your life, there is a great deal of joy to be experienced at that moment—if you only take the time to realize it. Of course, gratitude is one of the keys to feeling joy and enjoying each day—gratitude for good health, a warm home, a husband who cares, parents who still keep helping, and children who have their own opinions.

Don't misunderstand me. I'm not saying that every moment should be just filled with joy; that is simply not possible. I realized this one Christmas when I was coping with the fact that preparing for Christmas was not the "every-day-more-exciting-and-wonderful" scenario I had envisioned from the storybooks. Especially when the two-year-old opens all the presents on December twenty-first and a couple of kids get diarrhea or croup to add to the holiday cheer. The real joy of Christmas comes in a few special moments when, for example, you watch your six little dears really put their hearts into singing "O Come, All Ye Faithful" on somebody else's doorstep, or you see the joy in Jonah's face as he hands Talmadge the gift he has bought with his own hard-earned money. These moments make all the quarrels, wasted Scotch tape, food dribbled down the cupboard doors, and endless hours of shopping and preparing fade into one big lump of "necessary hazards," and those ten or twelve really special sets of moments stand out like beacons!

Every week has those special moments, if we just watch for them. It is too easy to dwell on the negative and not even see the positive, let alone comment on it. How often do we go into a playroom and say, "I love the way you two are playing nicely together," as opposed to the number of times we become angry over quarrels or misbehavior and yell, "Okay, you guys, who did this!"

Make a conscious effort to be positive. Tell your children the things you appreciate and like about them. They often don't even realize those things! Compliment them on putting toys away or getting homework done without being told, instead of just expecting it or nagging at them when they don't.

William James said, "The deepest principle of human nature is the craving to be appreciated." Think of the nice little things your children have done today—things you so often take for granted.

A friend gave me a great idea: "I go into the children's rooms every night that I'm home to tuck them in," she began. "I make a conscious effort when I walk into each room to turn off all the problems and 'negatives' of the day and turn my mind to something that that child has done that day that was helpful or admirable. Sometimes that's really hard, but even if the deed is only tiny, I tell him about it. Sincere appreciation and compliments go a long way. They "calm the savage beast" and inspire the child to do something even better tomorrow.

Little things—kindnesses, sharing, obedience—frequently slip past without being mentioned. When we let this happen, we lose a golden opportunity to let our children know that we think they're terrific, in spite of any minor flaws they may possess.

## Keep Reminding Yourself How Much Fun You're Having

Amidst whines and wails of a hard afternoon, and after five days of being without Richard, I looked up to see him pull in the driveway and start to unload presents from the back of his car.

It seemed that those five days of being mother and father had been full of hard decisions, such as not letting Saydi stay overnight with a friend because the last time she had stayed up all night and had been unbearable for three days afterward. Heartbroken, she had bawled like a sick cow and in her own feisty way was heard to say under her breath as she stomped off to her room to get over it, "I never knew you could be so mean!"

I had spent that afternoon "cracking the whip" to see that responsibilities, practicing, and homework were done. A special urgency hung in the air as we all anticipated making everything look nice for Daddy.

As I watched him walk in, laden with little gifts and grinning ear to ear, my first thought was how nice it was to have him back. My second thought, however, was: "Well, here comes Santa Claus! I do all the hard stuff and he comes home and has a ball!"

We can get hung up on that attitude if we're not careful: He gets to walk away from the mess every day to a nice, orderly office and I run from one disaster to the next.

On another occasion, a cold January morning, I was feeling particularly sorry for myself. Richard had been gone for a week. He was preparing the way for our move back to our Washington, D.C., residence, to which we were returning because he had accepted the chairmanship of the White House Conference for

Parents and Children. It was inauguration time, and every night he called on the phone with a glowing report of the spectacular fireworks at the Lincoln Memorial, or his meeting with the Secretary of HEW or the wonderful inaugural balls (don't worry, nobody dances, they only stand shoulder to shoulder and look at each other's party clothes).

On the afternoon of the big parade, I sat excitedly on top of the packing boxes with my nose pressed to the TV. I was sure that I would see him as the Utah delegation approached the presidential stand. Just as the announcer heralded their coming, the phone rang and I missed the whole thing. Tired and bitter, I distinctly remember thinking, "He gets to have all the fun."

Early that evening, as I had promised, the children piled in the car and, in spite of lightly falling snow, we began to hand-deliver birthday invitations for our two children whose birthdays were within a few days of each other. They insisted that they wanted to give the invitations to their friends personally, and that just receiving them in the mail wasn't nearly as much fun, especially when they all lived in the neighborhood. Eighteen invitations were stuffed in their hot little hands, and after the first two or three I thought to myself, *You must be crazy! It's a cold, miserable winter night and you're running up and down these hills like an ant who's lost his way.*

The children always went in different combinations of two, according to whose friend it was and who hadn't recently had a turn. After four or five doors I noticed something very interesting. When the duo turned from the door after placing an invitation in the hands of a friend or mother or sister, their faces were literally aglow with pleasure! They had made someone happy, and their joy shone in their faces.

After a few more doors I forgot all my woes and watched for their joyful expressions. The grins never failed. I was so sorry that Richard was not there to see it. As that thought passed through my mind, I realized that I was really the one who was having fun! I was watching happiness ooze from our children because they were making their friends happy. What could be better? When Richard got home he agreed. He told the children how much he had missed them and how much he preferred their company to the president's!

We mothers do have fun watching these little ones learn and grow. Sometimes we're so close that we can't see it, so we have to step back a little and focus—and remind ourselves about how much fun we're having!

Not long ago Richard was speaking to a large audience and decided to try an experiment. He asked all those with eight or more children to stand. There were seven couples who rose. One had sixteen (a combination of yours, mine, and ours), one fourteen, one eleven, and so on. He asked each couple to describe one moment that they remembered most vividly when they had felt a great amount of joy as a family.

All of the answers were extremely interesting and insightful, but the one that I was most impressed by was given by a beautiful silver-haired woman who stood by herself. "I don't know exactly what to say," she said. "We raised eight sons and every day was pure joy! I guess the moment that stands out most clearly may sound a little strange. It occurred while I was standing with all eight sons around the casket of my husband on the day of his funeral. I looked at those good, strong, loving sons and felt more joy than I had ever known. I realized that we had made it, my husband and I. We had raised eight wonderful people who were actively contributing to the betterment of their own families, their church, and their community."

I was touched by her feelings, but as much as I appreciated what she was saying, I was stunned by her first statement: *"Every day was pure joy."* I couldn't say that every one of my days was sheer joy by any means, and we don't even have all boys! What was I doing wrong?

As she continued to talk, it dawned on me. She had forgotten! There had to have been hard days: trials, sickness, and even a little rebelling, but when it was all over and she had done her best—and been successful—she forgot the bad times and remembered only the joy. I think there is a lesson in that for all of us. As we get older we tend to forget the hard times and replace them with the good—something wonderful to look forward to!

When our oldest child turned twelve, I underwent a definite mothering crisis. The children were growing up! *Someday these children will walk out the door on their own. They will "fly the coop." Someday I won't be changing diapers anymore, except for the grandchildren's,* I thought.

Although it seems impossible, someday we'll be able to walk across the kitchen floor in slippers without picking up a quarter cup of crumbs, water, dried peas, and smushed apple on our spongy soles. Someday we'll be able to find all the brushes and pens and scissors we want, and we'll be able to walk into the kitchen without saying, "Shut the fridge door!" An end will come to the days of standing over the plumber, wringing our hands, and saying, "I can't imagine what the baby's thrown in there this time!"

Before we can believe it has happened, the children will be grown and gone. I'm sure there is a different kind of joy in being grandparents—and even maybe extended periods of "the mess" from grandchildren—but it's not the same.

We might have joy rides like the grandpas and grandmas in the old cars, but we must remember that most of them returned home that afternoon to empty houses and only the memory of how well they did as parents while they were "in the fire."

Love every moment and try to visualize each day as an exciting adventure—because tomorrow, it will be gone!

CHALLENGES

1. Make a list of your blessings and program your mind to arise each morning with a sense of adventure rather than of doom.

2. Decide on a certain time and/or place each day to express your sincere appreciation and love to your husband and children. Try it for just one week and see if it doesn't shock your family into more loving and thoughtful patterns.

3. Look for those special little incidents during the week that remind you that *you* are the one who is really having all the fun! Record those special moments in your journal. Some of them might be classified as "disasters" to begin with, but remember the formula "crisis plus time equals humor."

# Chapter 8

# You Can Change

After leading a parenting workshop one evening, Richard and I were approached by a young mother. "Do you ever get discouraged?" she blurted out to me. Her eyes were so full of water that one blink made the tears spill over, try as she did to keep them in. Embarrassed, she tried to flip them away, but they just kept spilling out.

I put my arm around her and remembered having felt that way so many times. "How many children do you have, and how old is your littlest one?" I asked.

"I have six children," she said as she swallowed hard. "The oldest one is seven and the baby is three months." I smiled knowingly and said, "Don't worry, things will get better. The answer to your question is unequivocally yes. Nothing can make you feel more humble and helpless than a pack of little kids." (Even one little one can do a pretty good job!)

We commiserated for a few minutes. I shed a tear or two myself, and she went away smiling, but still sniffing.

I thought about her occasionally during the next few months and even used her example in talking to other mothers to assure them that we all get discouraged. Then, a few months later, after another seminar, I looked up and there she was again. "Remember me?" she asked with a big smile. "I'm the one who was gushing with tears the last time I saw you!"

I felt a real love for her as we began talking again. During the course of the conversation she said: "You know, sometimes I say to myself, 'Why am I doing this to myself? I chose to have these children, but they're destroying my free agency! I never get to do anything I want to do. My time is totally occupied with feeding and clothing, changing and cajoling, trying to get kids to practice and put their things away, quit fighting and be kind to one another.' Then," she went on, "I realize something very interesting every time as I get to the end of that tirade: I am the one who is benefiting from it all. I have to change. In order to survive, I have to train my mind to do things I know I should. I can feel myself becoming a little more patient and understanding. I learn how to cope with my anger and I begin to feel the true love of Christ as I watch these children learn to love each other.

"Now that my oldest has turned eight and has really started to help in a meaningful way, I can see the light at the end of the tunnel. Even though it is very difficult, I'm beginning to see that the Lord answered my prayers in giving me these children so that *I* could grow and learn and refine myself."

As she walked away, I couldn't help but think of another mother I had spoken to the night before. She had just taken a full-time job. "It's so wonderful to get out of that messy house and away from my screaming, demanding little preschoolers," she said. "They love it with the baby sitter and I get a chance to meet so many stimulating people! I'm learning things about computers that I never knew existed!"

Again came the stark realization that the real truth is exactly the opposite of what some factions of the women's movement imply. The place where we can improve and refine ourselves most drastically—if we accept the challenge—is at home.

## Overcoming Weaknesses

Progress means change. The times we grow the most are those times when we are required to change something we don't like about ourselves.

I heard a Sunday School lesson a few years ago that impressed me a great deal. The teacher pointed out that we often think of repentance as a long, drawn-out process that includes five steps and a lot of time. When the Savior of mankind asked us to repent, I don't think he meant it to apply only to the murderers and adulterers. He meant it to apply to us: everyday mothers with problems to work out.

In my opinion, the Savior's most adamant request, next to loving God and our fellowmen, was to *repent*. Repentance involves change.

Children provide us with many great blessings. One is the absolute need to change in order to survive. A wise man once said, "If you want to be a better parent, change yourself before you try to change your children."

One of life's greatest dangers is the statement: "I know I shouldn't be that way but I can't help it. I'd like to be different but I just can't. That's just the way I am. I can't change."

In Ether 12:27 we find a very wonderful insight and promise from the Lord: "And if [women] come unto me I will show unto them their weakness. I give unto [women] weakness that they may be humble; and my grace is sufficient for all [women] that humble themselves before me; for if they humble themselves before me, and have faith in me, then will I make weak things become strong unto them."

What a revelation! We are given weaknesses on purpose so that we can be humble! And when we are humble (knowing that we can't do anything without the Lord's help, but also knowing that we can do everything with that help) and we have the faith that he will help us, then our weaknesses truly become our greatest strengths!

With that concept in mind, we can't say: "I'm not a good mother because I'm just not patient. My mother was very impatient and I inherited that trait. I just can't cope with things when my children are naughty. I fly off the handle and do and say things that I regret when it's all over. That's just the way I am."

I must admit that the hair raises a little on the back of my neck when someone says to me, "You're the perfect person to have a large family. You're so patient and calm all the time."

In the first place, that is not true. I still become irritated and impatient and uptight with the children much too often, but I am enjoying working on it even though it's the hardest job I have.

It is very comforting to know that we all have a set of weaknesses to work with, and that if we really believe that we can change those weaknesses, they can actually become our strengths.

A young mother tells the story of looking down one morning just in time to see her one-year-old chomping down the last of a bottle of multivitamins with iron. Her story goes like this:

"I just laid him down, poured Ipecac down him to make it come back up, put him in the bathtub with a couple of washable toys, and read a story to him while I sat on the toilet waiting for him to throw up. After three 'upchucks' I counted twenty vitamins still intact and there was so much bright pink that I knew lots had dissolved. I thanked Heavenly Father for Ipecac and his help to keep me calm, and loaded my three preschoolers in the van to run an errand. As I whizzed along the freeway I heard the baby saying, 'bah-bah,' and I looked in the rearview mirror to see him pointing out the back window with a sock in one hand and a shoe in the other. The other sock and shoe were gone, and I realized that he'd been throwing everything he could find (which was a lot) out the back window.

"Once again I mustered up my calmness, pulled the van over to the side of the road, went back and retrieved a sandal that had miraculously lodged in the spare tire on the outside, and squinted my eyes to see a bottle or shoe or any other household items on the road. Seeing none, and realizing that there was no going back and no malice intended, I got back in the van and giggled all the way to the store.

"Five years ago I would have died over that morning, but I realized on that particular occasion that after many years of working hard to remain calm even in disastrous situations, my weakness was becoming my strength. I was able to handle it with surprising ease. Heavenly Father is really helping me!"

This same scripture applies to a time in my own life when I almost let my weakness—fear—destroy a gift I'd been given.

My parents spent what seemed like half of their small income on music lessons for me, not to mention the untold hours of

coaxing, pleading, cajoling, threatening, and encouraging me to
practice—and carting me back and forth to lessons. However,
when it came to performing, I was so frightened that the people
who heard me play my violin wondered whether the technique
of shaking the left hand to create a vibrato also carried through
to the right hand as my bow trembled and bounced down the
string on the wings of my utter fear.

I kept thinking it would get better. My sister and I were the
only two violinists in the entire Bear Lake valley and it seemed
that we played for almost every funeral, wedding reception,
church meeting, or party ever held in the county. The degrees of
fright varied, but these were always emotionally draining experiences for me.

When I went to college, I decided to major in music. *Surely
that will change things*, I thought. I did love music, and I knew
that Heavenly Father had given me a special gift, but when it
came to performing, things seemed to get worse. I continued to
practice hard but avoided performances whenever possible—and
so often felt devastated when I had to perform, and fear kept me
from doing my best.

When I married and opportunities arose again to play—
mostly because my crazy husband kept telling people that I was a
concert violinist—I finally came to the point where I had to
decide if the agony I went through each time I played was really
worth it, or if I should just eliminate the stress and quit playing.

I'll never forget the soul searching I went through in trying
to make that decision. As I was sorting things out, with
Richard's help, I found a scripture that stated, "Perfect love
casteth out fear." (1 John 4:18.) *Perfect love for whom?* I thought.
*Love for music, love for God, or love for myself?* To make a long
story short, I decided that it was all three. I decided to use my
mind in a different way when I played. Instead of worrying about
making a mistake, or worrying that people must think I was
really smart because I could play the violin, or worrying that my
slip was showing, I started thinking how much I loved the music
I was playing and how much I wanted to portray its beauty to
the audience. I thought of how much I loved my Heavenly

Father for giving me a way to express my feelings through music, and how much I appreciated the audience for listening to my contribution. With those feelings, along with a special blessing from my husband, I could feel myself progressing.

Although it's still hard for me to control my thoughts at times, I can see that I have really changed. One of my greatest weaknesses is beginning to be a strength. Now I can honestly say that one of the greatest joys in my life is to play in a string quartet or duet or yes, even occasionally a solo!

One of the most glorious things about being a mother is the potential for personal growth. You don't have to go on not liking things about yourself. You can set a goal and work on a plan to grow and progress and work out the kinks in your personality. You can have all the traits necessary to develop the greatest quality of all: charity—the pure love of Christ.

This quality is even more important than faith and hope, the scriptures tell us. Here is the definition: "Charity suffereth long, and is kind; charity envieth not; charity vaunteth not itself, is not puffed up. Doth not behave itself unseemly, seeketh not her own, is not easily provoked, thinketh no evil; Rejoiceth not in iniquity, but rejoiceth in the truth; Beareth all things, believeth all things, hopeth all things, endureth all things." (1 Corinthians 13:4-7.)

I challenge anyone to find a better definition of a good mother.

Charity really is attainable if we work on perfecting little things—or big things—one step at a time. Decide weekly or monthly what you'd like to change, and work on it. We can all be like Benjamin Franklin, who worked on one concept about himself each month that he wanted to improve, to change, from "being prompt" to "enjoying nature." Soon that good habit becomes part of us and we can begin to work on the next while keeping the last on retainer.

You can change! You can become the person you were created to be—and that exhilarating feeling of "becoming" is unparalleled in any other earthly experience. The harder it is, the more rewarding the success.

## The Last Great Challenge

Analyze the things that you know you should change about yourself. (If you have trouble coming up with something, ask your children.) Make a list (keep it short—even *one* thing will be plenty for now).

Then use all your understanding and capability to come up with a workable plan, and start to change. Use the principles of analyzing your situation, deciding in advance, holding Sunday Sessions, and making a commitment to someone else.

With the help of a strong commitment, a real desire and a loving Heavenly Father who wants you to succeed, you can do it.

You can become the mother you want to be. With the proper planning and desire you can learn to cope with stress, to remain calm, to set proper priorities, and to put your life in order. You can spend precious quality time with each child and your husband and expand your own horizons. You can do it! And by doing so you become, in the truest sense, "a joyful mother of children."

# Index

(cont.)

⑨ Window deeds –
       – "see the needs of another"
                 look thru window
     ( within / outside of our own
                         family )
  ✝ most window deeds are small
             but appreciated.

⑩ Family partnership c̄ God


Discuss why it's important to
      keep learning / refining ourselves.

3/93

My plans for change: DeeAnn —

40
① Prepare dinner in the morning —
    a) alleviate hurrying at dinner time / tired
    b) available to Patrick after school — "not busy"

② Chart? (Shared chores) *Responsibility
    • reread Teaching Child. Responsib.

③ Plan for the day / week? / *month?
("sharpening your saw" pg. 44)
    — become more organized / success at
               completing tasks

\* 5 - facet review:
    mental, physical, social, emotionally
               and spiritually

④ Continue to simplify house / garage
    and daily schedule!
    Patrick: put away toys / store ones that
        aren't your favorite.
    all: Sat., prepare for Sunday.
    all: "all in one movement" — putting
           things away ….

⑤ Learn together — read,
a) Read ensign ⟩    study a subject a
   friend / together   month (art for ex.)
   a topic a     Decide start of month
   day?

⑥ Flexibility —

⑦ Dating — all / 1:1
        mommy dates, daddy - dates …

⑧ Goal planning — Sundays for the week